With Best Wishes for a
Happy Birthday -

With love from

Bee & Anne.

1944.

A
HISTORY OF
EVERYDAY THINGS
IN ENGLAND

A Note on the Methods and Influence of the QUENNELLS on History Teaching

By FRANK ROSCOE, M.A.

Secretary of the Royal Society of Teachers

THE subject of history has formed part of the school curriculum for several generations, but it is only during recent years that any serious attempt has been made to enliven it with material likely to interest the young. A century ago schools began the practice of treating the dates of events as all-important while giving little attention to the events themselves. In the later middle of last century there were text-books ambitious in scope but unattractive in form and content. They treated history mainly as a record of dynasties, wars and conquests, ignoring the lives and doings of ordinary men and women.

John Richard Green saw the defects of this kind of treatment, and wrote his " Short History of the English People " as a corrective and an example. His work was extremely useful, but the beneficial influence was limited in the main to students of mature years.

The ever-widening scope of historical research has opened many different fields of study. We have to-day many " histories "—ancient, modern, political, social, local, economic, religious or literary, with countless specialised branches such as the history of architecture, of shipping, of games, localities or buildings. Amid this vast and ill-ordered mass of facts, all falling under the general title " history," some guidance must be given to the young student. Lacking a coherent thread or clue he may be engulfed in confusion, unable to see the wood for the trees.

The most vivid and striking contribution to the new method of treating history for young students was devised by C. H. B. Quennell, in happy collaboration with his wife, Marjorie Quennell. Neither of them had been through the conventional discipline of historical study and research. She is an artist by training and inclination ; he was an architect to whom the last War brought an interruption of a successful professional career. His chief interest was in architecture, and in the course of his practice he developed an abiding zest for examples of good workmanship, and a profound respect for skilled craftsmen in every field. His desire to convey something of his own knowledge and enthusiasm was the mainspring of his efforts in authorship. Beginning with the charming volumes entitled "A History of Everyday Things in England " (Batsford), he and Mrs. Quennell went on to describe everyday things at different periods and in different places.

It is hardly too much to say that they made history while writing it. By laborious research and careful selection they were able to present the story of people " in their habit as they lived." Skilful illustrations supplemented the text, and the effect was strengthened by the fortunate choice of a publisher whose skill in the production of books goes far beyond the practice of the maker of cheap " best-sellers." This happy conjunction of author, artist and publisher furnished a memorable and permanent contribution to the list of books available for young students of history. The general run of school text-books might be described as drab in appearance and in contents, but the Quennell books are attractive and even exhilarating in both respects. We need not wonder that they are finding imitators and helping to raise the standard of book-production for schools.

Quennell's chief characteristic was an unquenchable enthusiasm for things that are " beautiful and of good report." He would journey for miles to see a well-built farm wagon or any good example of handicraft. He had about him no trace of self-assurance nor any of the windy rhetoric used by self-styled connoisseurs on art or architecture.

In the memory of those who knew him, C. H. B. Quennell has an assured place. They will always be able to recall vivid pictures of one who radiated goodwill towards his fellows, treating their failings with whimsical humour and extracting merriment from circumstances untoward enough to have discouraged a spirit less well armed against fate. He had a blithe heart and an unfailing zest for simple human joys. Children loved him, the sure perception of youth enabling them to see in him one who was ready to share their interests without assuming the airs of a mentor. This firm link with childhood was of a piece with the man, for he retained to the end the inquiring spirit and quick enthusiasms of youth. He died on December 5, 1935. A fitting epitaph for him might be found in the words of Robert Louis Stevenson :

" Every heart that has beat strong and cheerfully has left a hopeful impulse behind it in the world, and bettered the condition of mankind."

FIG. 1.—The Village Fair. (Details of Merry-go-round from a sketch made by Heywood Sumner in 1892.)

A
HISTORY OF
EVERYDAY THINGS
IN ENGLAND
DONE IN FOUR PARTS
OF WHICH
THIS IS THE FOURTH
THE AGE OF
PRODUCTION
1851-1942.
SECOND EDITION, *Revised*

FOOD · RAIL-WAYS · CLOTHES · MACHINERY · SANITATION · TRANSPORT · HOUSES

Written and Illustrated by
MARJORIE and C.H.B.QUENNELL
Published by
B.T.BATSFORD LTD LONDON

Pasteur described himself as "a man whose invincible belief is that Science and Peace will triumph over Ignorance and War, that nations will unite, not to destroy, but to build, and that the future will belong to those who will have done most for suffering humanity."

THIS BOOK IS DEDICATED BY ITS AUTHORS
TO THE MEMORY OF
THE THREE FRIENDS

WILLIAM MORRIS
POET ARCHITECT DESIGNER
WEAVER SOCIAL REFORMER & PRINTER

EDWARD BURNE-JONES
PAINTER & DESIGNER

&

PHILIP WEBB
ARCHITECT & FINE DRAUGHTSMAN

WHO
CONTRIBUTED LARGELY TO THE ALTERATION OF THE
APPEARANCE OF EVERYDAY THINGS
DURING THE NINETEENTH CENTURY

First published Autumn 1934
Second Edition, Winter 1941–2

MADE AND PRINTED IN GREAT BRITAIN FOR THE PUBLISHERS, B. T. BATSFORD LTD.,
LONDON AND MALVERN WELLS, BY THE TONBRIDGE PRINTERS LTD., TONBRIDGE

PREFATORY NOTE

THE boys and girls for whom we write will know, from their history lessons, that as a period recedes it is much easier to get a general picture of it than of events which are quite recent. In the same way the archæologists have discovered that the earthworks on the Downs, which are puzzling when viewed on the ground, resolve themselves into a logical plan when viewed in the air from an aeroplane. How are we to give a general picture of this period to the present day?

In 1851 our grandfathers and great-grandfathers doubtless thought that all that remained was to set the machine to work and live off its products peacefully and quietly—but the machines bred other machines, each speedier than the last, and peace and quietness disappeared. Again, the machine made more goods than were necessary to supply the local demands, so foreign markets had to be discovered ; then foreign raw materials had to be taken in exchange. Unheard-of complexities and jealousies were introduced into trade. Enormous additional charges were necessary for packing, retailing and distributing.

Still the picture is there—if we have but the eyes to see it. In our attempt we have given most attention to the three great primary trades, and have shown how man fed, housed and clothed himself in these years. These are, after all, the great essentials. In the space at our command we have only been able to touch on his other activities and mention a few of the many interesting developments. We have given these in their chronological order of appearance, and if this is a little confusing then it is only like life itself in our period. No sooner had people got used to one invention than another appeared which upset the apple-cart. Our readers can search for our omissions, and then submit them to a test : Is this, that, or the other thing, an essential? This questioning is going on all over the world to-day, and it constitutes a revolution. We like our revolutions in this country to be peaceful ones, so if we can bring ourselves to regard certain changes as being necessary, then, with courage, we may be able to build a worthier fabric of civilization. It is, after all, more interesting to live in a period that is alive than one which suffers from a fatty degeneration of its soul.

These are the points which we think should be remembered. We can grow all the foodstuffs we require, and mine for coal and iron. Man has invented the most wonderful production plant. With its aid he can produce all that he requires—the production problem is settled. The real question is—What do we propose to do with the plenty which Providence has placed at our disposal ? It is distribution which comes to the fore now. If, as Pasteur said, " the nations will unite, not to destroy, but to build," then we can very speedily free the world from hunger and want. But if the nations continue to turn their thoughts to destruction, we shall be courting disaster. It will be said of us that we did not know how to build, and our names will be bracketed with the greatest failure in history.

MARJORIE and C. H. B. QUENNELL.

BERKHAMPSTEAD, Herts, 1934.

v

NOTE TO SECOND EDITION

The call for the second edition comes in the midst of the fierce and ruthless second world war, when Mrs. Marjorie Quennell is in the United States of America, where she is slowly recovering from a severe and prolonged illness.   C. H. B. Quennell died just over a year after the book's first publication.   In these circumstances it has seemed advisable to re-issue the work with a comparatively slight revision, only replacing such passages as recent developments or war conditions had rendered obsolete.
WINTER 1941-2   THE PUBLISHERS

NOTE OF ACKNOWLEDGMENT

WE wish to acknowledge our indebtedness to the following ladies, gentlemen and firms who have so kindly helped us with information :

ON MORRIS, BURNE-JONES and WEBB : Prof. J. W. Mackail ; Miss Emery Walker ; Dr. A. H. Horsfall ; Messrs. Longmans Green & Co. Ltd. ; H. C. Marillier ; C. C. Winmill ; H. J. L. J. Massé ; Sydney C. Cockerell ; Powell & Sons Ltd. ; H. F. T. Cooper ; and Morris & Co. Ltd. for the engravings of the colour plates of Morris fabrics.

ON THE PUBLIC HEALTH : A. F. Bean ; M. L. Tildesley ; Sir D'Arcy Power ; Kenneth M. B. Cross ; George Jennings Ltd. ; Dr. L. W. G. Malcolm ; W. H. Rudd.

ON BUILDING : J. M. Sturgess ; W. H. Godfrey ; Sir Giles Gilbert Scott ; C. F. A. Voysey ; E. J. May ; Wells Coates and Pleydell-Bouverie ; W. H. Collin ; Barry Parker and Sir Raymond Unwin ; F.R.I.B.A. ; Erich Mendelsohn and Serge Chermayeff ; Walter Millard ; Messrs. Adams, Holden and Pearson ; Prof. A. E. Richardson ; H. de C. Hastings and S. Bylander ; First Garden City Ltd. ; *The Architects' Journal* ; *The Architect and Building News* ; London Passenger Transport Board ; London, Midland & Scottish Railway Company ; Building Centre Ltd.

ON FURNITURE : Sir Ambrose Heal ; H. H. Peach ; A. K. Sabin ; Radio Pictures Ltd.

ON TRANSPORT : Capt. W. H. Dowman ; J. Dixon-Scott ; Morris Motors Ltd., Cowley, for the engravings in colour of the Assembly Lines in the Morris works, drawn for them by Bryan de Grineau, *The Motor* artist, arranged by Service Advertising Co. Ltd. and published in *The Autocar*.

ON SOCIAL LIFE : The Salvation Army.

ON FOOD : The Canadian Government ; J. Raymond ; Messrs. Spillers Ltd. ; Messrs. Henry Simon Ltd. ; the Aerated Bread Co. Ltd. ; Messrs. J. Lyons and Co. Ltd. ; Messrs. Burrell & Sons, of Glasgow ; Messrs. Shaw Savill and Albion Co. Ltd.

ON PRODUCTION AND DISTRIBUTION : Albert Kahn ; Morris Motors Ltd ; Hubert Courtney ; Co-operative Wholesale Society Ltd. ; W. K. Wallace ; Army and Navy Co-operative Society Ltd. ; Civil Service Supply Association Ltd.

CONTENTS

It should be mentioned that since the first edition was issued, the Red House at Bexley has again changed hands.

Kings and Political	Social
	1846 Repeal of Corn Laws begins Free Trade
1848 Year of revolutions and Chartists	1848 First Public Health Acts and cholera epidem
	1849 Bedford College, London, founded
	1850 Ebenezer Howard born
1851 QUEEN VICTORIA	
1852 Louis Napoleon becomes Napoleon III	1852 Death of Duke of Wellington
1854–6 Crimean War	1854 Cholera epidemic
	Cheltenham College for Girls
	Florence Nightingale starts nursing
1857–9 Indian Mutiny	
	1858 Formation of Volunteers
1859–61 War of Italian Unity	1859 William Morris marries Jane Burden
	1859–65 Mrs. Beeton's cookery book
1861–5 American Civil War	1861 Death of Prince Consort
	1862 A.B.C. starts business
	" Unto This Last " (Ruskin)
	1863 Henry Ford born
1864 Schleswig-Holstein taken by Prussia.	1864 Garibaldi visits England
1865 Assassination of President Lincoln	1865 Foundation of Salvation Army
Austro-Prussian War	
	1868 Dulwich College (Charles Barry)
1870 Franco-Prussian War, Republic in France, and	1870 Education Act (Compulsory)
Empire in Germany.	Ruskin Slade Professor at Oxford
	1872 Charterhouse School (Hardwick)
	Girls' Public Day Schools Company
	Girton College, Cambridge, founded
	1875 Newnham College, Cambridge, founded
	Foundation Grosvenor Gallery
1877 Queen Victoria becomes Empress of India	1877 Foundation of Society for Protection of Ancie
	Buildings
1879 Zulu War	1878 Whistler v. Ruskin libel action
1881 Boer War. Majuba	1880 Bedford Park Estate developed
1882 Murder of Lord Frederick Cavendish	1882 St. Paul's School, Hammersmith (Waterhouse
	Death of Rossetti
	1883 Foundation Boys' Brigade
1884 Grab for Africa begins	1884 Foundation Toynbee Hall
	Foundation Fabian Society
	Foundation Art Workers' Guild
1886 Gladstone's Home Rule Bill	1885 Death of General Gordon
	1887 " Looking Backward " (Bellamy)
	Queen Victoria's Jubilee
	Foundation Arts and Crafts Ex. Society
	1889 Great dock strike for dockers' "tanner" an ho
1890	Booth's " Life and Labour of People of London
	1891 Education Act (Free)
	1894 Christ's Hospital, Horsham (Webb and Bell)
1895 Jameson Raid	
	1896 Death of William Morris
	1897 Diamond Jubilee
1898 Fashoda incident	1898 " To-morrow " (Ebenezer Howard)
Battle of Omdurman	
1899–1902 S. African War	
1900 German Navy Law	1900 Death of Ruskin
1901 EDWARD VII. Boxer Rebellion	1901 Beginning of Boy Scouts
1903 Chamberlain's Tariff Reform	
1904–5 Russo-Japanese War	
1906 Self-government S. Africa	
50 Labour Members returned to Parliament	
	1909 John Burns' Town-Planning Act
1910 GEORGE V	
1911 Parliament Act	
1914–18 Great War	1928 Death of Ebenezer Howard

Science and Industry	The Arts
	1848 Formation of Pre-Raphaelite Brotherhood
	1849 Publication of " Seven Lamps of Architecture " by John Ruskin
851 First cable to Calais	
The Great Exhibition in Hyde Park	
	1853 Publication of Ruskin's " Stones of Venice "
854 Crystal Palace rebuilt at Sydenham	1854 Holman Hunt's " Light of the World " at R.A.
56 Working Men's College in Great Ormond Street	1856 W. P. Frith's (1819-1909) " Derby Day "
Perkin discovered aniline dyes	Balliol Chapel (Butterfield)
	Rossetti's " Annunciation "
	Holman Hunt's " Scapegoat "
857 Pasteur's paper on Fermentation	1857 Wellington Memorial (Alfred Stevens)
858 First cable to America	
859 Darwin's " Origin of Species "	1859 Philip Webb designs Red House for Morris
863 Foundation Co-operative Wholesale Society	
864 London sewerage system	1864 Albert Memorial (G. G. Scott)
865 New cable to America	
Mechanical vehicles four miles an hour	1866 St. Pancras Station, London (G. G. Scott)
866 New American cable	" Alice in Wonderland "
867 Lister at work	1867 Street wins Law Courts, London, competition
Monier's patent for reinforced concrete	
869 Opening of Suez Canal	
870 Tramways Act	
871 Prince of Wales (Edward VII) caught typhoid fever. As a result modern sanitary system evolved by Chadwick, Corfield, Field and Hellyer	1872 " Alice Through the Looking Glass "
874 London School of Medicine for Women	1875 St. Agnes', Kennington (G. G. Scott, jun.)
Ruskin makes undergraduates build roads	" Trial by Jury " (Gilbert and Sullivan)
876 Koch begins work	" The Sorcerer " (Gilbert and Sullivan)
Bell's telephones	
Pelton hydraulic turbine	
879 Foundation of Bournville Garden City	1878 " H.M.S. Pinafore "
880 First cargo of frozen beef from Australia	1880 " Pirates of Penzance "
	1881 " Patience "
882 First cargo of frozen mutton from New Zealand	1882 " Iolanthe "
	} Gilbert & Sullivan
884 Gold discovered on the Rand	1884 " Ida "
Daimler invents motor engine	
Parsons invents steam turbine	
885 Carl Benz builds his motor-car	1885 " Mikado "
	About 1886 Constitutional Club, London (Edis)
	1887 Competition for Imperial Institute won by T. E. Collcutt
888 Dunlop tyre patent	1888 " Plain Tales from the Hills " (Kipling)
Foundation Port Sunlight Garden City	" Yeomen of the Guard " } Gilbert & Sullivan
Nansen crosses Greenland	1889 " Gondoliers "
890 First Tube railway and Forth Bridge	About 1890 New Scotland Yard (Norman Shaw)
892 Diesel engine patented	About 1892 Beginning of Westminster Cathedral (R.C.) (Bentley)
893 Ford's first car	1893 Utopia Ltd.
	1894 Du Maurier's " Trilby " in Harper's
895 Rontgen discovers X-rays	
896 Mechanical vehicles twelve miles an hour	
897 Ronald Ross discovers malarial parasite	1897 Kipling's " Recessional "
Marconi experiments with wireless	
	1900 Competition for new Sessions House, London (E. W. Mountford)
	1901 Competition for Victoria Memorial won by Aston Webb
903 Mechanical vehicles twenty miles an hour	1903 First garden city, at Letchworth, begun
Foundation first garden city, Letchworth	Giles G. Scott wins Liverpool Cathedral competition
Dec. 17th. The Wright brothers make the first mechanically propelled flight in an aeroplane	
	1905 Wesleyan Hall, Westminster, competition won by Lanchester and Rickards
909 Blériot flies the Channel	
920 Foundation second garden city, Welwyn	

SHORT LIST OF AUTHORITIES

Life of William Morris. J. W. MACKAIL. (Longmans, 1922.)

Memorials of Edward Burne-Jones. By G. B.-J. (Macmillan, 1904.)

Three Houses. ANGELA THIRKELL. (Oxford University Press, 1931.)

William Morris and His Art. LEWIS F. DAY. *Easter Art Annual*, 1899.

A History of the Frozen Meat Trade. CRITCHELL and RAYMOND. (Constable, 1912.)

Record of Seasons' Prices. T. H. BAKER. (Simpkin, Marshall & Co.)

Reports of the Food Investigation Boards. (H.M. Stationery Office.)

Agricultural Implements and Machinery. SPENCER and PASSMORE. (Science Museum, 1930.)

Land Everlasting. A. G. STREET. (John Lane, 1934.)

Town-Planning. RAYMOND UNWIN. (T. Fisher Unwin.)

Looking Backward. EDWARD BELLAMY. (William Reeves.)

To-morrow. E. HOWARD. (Swan, Sonnenschein & Co., 1898.)

Sir Ebenezer Howard. MACFADYEN. (Manchester University Press, 1933.)

Modern Public Baths and Wash-houses. A. W. S. and K. M. B. CROSS. (B. T. Batsford, 1903 and Simpkin Marshall Ltd., 1930.)

School Architecture. E. R. ROBSON. (John Murray, 1877.)

The Work of George Devey. WALTER H. GODFREY. (Batsford.)

Architectural Illustration Society. Published in *The Architect*, 1886–92, and *The Journal of the Royal Institute of British Architects*, *The Architects' Journal*, *Architectural Review*, *The Builder* and *Building News*.

The Story of the C.W.S. REDFERN. (Co-operative Wholesale Society.)

The Life of Pasteur. RENÉ VALLERY-RADOT. (Constable & Co., 1919.)

Main Drainage of London. HUMPHREYS. (Lond. Cty. Council, 1930.)

My Life and Work. HENRY FORD. (Heinemann, 1922.)

The Atlantic Telegraph. W. H. RUSSELL. (Day & Sons.)

Aeronautics. M. J. B. DAVY. (Science Museum, 1929.)

Land Transport, Parts 1, 2 and 3. E. A. FORWARD. (Science Museum, 1925, 1926 and 1931.)

Sailing Ships. G. S. LAIRD CLOWES. (Science Museum, 1930.)

Stationary Engines. H. W. DICKINSON. (Science Museum, 1925.)

Electric Power. W. T. O'DEA. (Science Museum, 1933.)

Water Transport. G. S. LAIRD CLOWES. (Science Museum, 1927.)

Traill's Social England. (Cassell & Co., 1904.)

John Leech's Pictures of Life and Character. (Bradbury, Agnew & Co., 1886, and *Punch*.)

Queen Victoria. LYTTON STRACHEY. (Chatto and Windus, 1921.)

Country Life, Illustrated London News, The Queen, Punch, Cornhill, etc.

Researches in the Application of Iron to Buildings. FAIRBAIRN (Longmans Green & Co., 1870.)

Modern Steelwork. W. R. GILBERT. (British Steelwork Assn., 1930.)

American Government and Culture. RUGG. (Ginn & Co., 1931.)

Costume. THALASSO CRUSO. (London Museum Catalogue, No. 5, and fashion journals noted on our drawings.)

CHAPTER I

A CURSORY CHRONICLE

1851–59

IT was in 1851 that William Morris, then a youth of seventeen, was taken to the Great Exhibition being held in Hyde Park, London. Who took him we do not know ; his mother perhaps—it could not have been his father, a respectable bill and discount broker in the City, who had died in 1847—but, whoever it was, here were all the beginnings and possibilities for a happy Victorian day. The Exhibition was the work of the Prince Consort, who despite much opposition had safely carried it through to a triumphant opening. The critics had been confounded, and the average Englishman, going to the Exhibition in its Crystal Palace, looked down the long vistas there and saw them continued, beyond reality, into the dreamland of a golden prosperity which was to continue for ever, with England as the workshop of the world. Mrs. Morris' breast may have swelled with some such feeling, if she it was who took William ; and then he spoiled the party by sitting down and refusing to go over the Exhibition, which he declared was " wonderfully ugly."

Here was a pretty kettle of fish for a Victorian mother. Boys, and girls for that matter, who do not react normally can be an infernal nuisance. You cannot very well smack a boy of seventeen, no matter how much you may want to, in the Entrance Hall of a Great Exhibition, nor is it a place in which one would willingly enter into a debate on the inwardness of ugliness. The point for us, however, is that, though it was a very bad beginning to a Victorian day, it was a very good beginning for William's life work. Morris was to be insurgent as well as artist, and the core of a group of men who were to kick against the pricks of all that the Great Exhibition stood for. There were amazing curiosities there to satisfy the populace, but the real god in the cella was the machine. Things had been

FIG. 2.—China Vase
(1851 Exhibition).

pretty bad in England. There had been famine in Ireland, and but for the repeal of the Corn Laws, in 1846, we might have had famine in England. The times had been troublous; 1848 was the year of wide-spread revolutions, and we had our own Chartists. So if the Exhibition was hateful to one group it was very hopeful to many others. The pity is, of course, that the two groups did not combine.

We dealt with the Great Exhibition and its exhibits in Vol. III, and tried to show how it was that people became so strangely insensitive to beauty in their scramble for wealth. Fig. 2 gives just one more reminder of the kind of things which were exhibited in 1851, and it may be that William saw this out of the tail of his eye, and so refused to be taken around. And this strange blight of ugliness was over everything. Architecture, the mother of the arts, was at its lowest ebb. All the gaiety of the Regency period had disappeared, and the monotony of Pimlico and Kensington had taken its place.

Morris was at Marlborough between 1848–51, and it was very different in those days from the public school of to-day. There were no organized games, so Morris employed his leisure in rambles through the country to study old churches and earthworks on the Downs. Even as a schoolboy he was developing his love of Gothic architecture.

The next step came when he went up to Oxford in 1852, and sat for the entrance examination in the Hall of Exeter, and it was a very important step, because the boy who sat next to him in the Hall was Edward Burne-Jones, the son and only child of a carver, gilder, and picture-framer in Birmingham. The two boys became friends— Burne-Jones was a year older than Morris, and the friendship so formed was to last throughout their lives. Carving, gilding and

Blue and white stripe silk dress lace collar   pleated bodice and skirt. Belt and sleeve bands of bright blue ribbon black edge.

FIG. 3.—London Museum (1851).

framing seems a more likely stock from which to breed an artist than discounting and bill broking, but the arts were not thought of for either of the boys, who were both destined for the Church.

Morris went up to Oxford in 1853, and his work there seems to have left him an ample leisure for study on his own lines. Ruskin's " Seven Lamps of Architecture " had been published in 1849, and the first part of his " The Stones of Venice " appeared in 1851, and Parts II and III in 1853. It was in Part II that the sixth chapter was devoted to a study of the " Nature of Gothic," and this one chapter can be taken as one of the formative influences of Morris' life. He always acknowledged it, and when later on, towards the end of his life, he set up his own Kelmscott Press, one of the first things he printed was the "Nature of Gothic."

Ruskin, who was born in 1819, was the son of a wealthy wine merchant, who travelled around selling sherry and took his boy with him. Ruskin went up to Christ Church, Oxford, when eighteen. His "Modern Painters" influenced Burne-Jones in much the same way that the "Nature of Gothic" did Morris, but the influence on the latter went deeper than its bearing on the decorative arts; it touched that inner spirit of Morris, the poet side which later was to send him viking to Iceland.

Once, when we were young, we saw Morris when he was old, and he seemed to us like one of the sea rovers of whom one reads in the "Burnt Njal Saga." When as a young man he read in the "Nature of Gothic,"—"And I believe this inquiry to be a pleasant and profitable one; and that there will be found something more than usually interesting in tracing out this grey, shadowy, many-pinnacled image of the Gothic spirit within us and discerning what fellowship there is between it and our Northern hearts,"—there can be no doubt that he was profoundly moved. You must be either Greek or Goth, and Morris was a Goth. We shall have more to say about this later on in our chapter on Building.

Another epoch-making date in Morris' life was 1855, when he and Burne-Jones went to France with Fulford, another friend. The glories of French Gothic were too much for our heroes; they went to France destined for the Church—they returned determined to be artists. Burne-Jones was to paint, and Morris to be an architect. So on January 21st, 1856, we find him entering the office of George Edmund Street, the architect to the Diocese of Oxford, who was then practising in Oxford. There he met Philip Webb, who was Street's head assistant, and was to become another lifelong friend. Webb, born 1831, was the son of an Oxford doctor. The friendship of these three men is told in Prof. J. W. Mackail's "Life of William Morris," and there was something very beautiful about it. They all came to-gether when they were young, which is the time to make friends ; they were all to become great, yet no one became too great for the others, and they were always meet-ing, and talking, and laughing, and play-ing practical jokes on one another. Burne-Jones was "Ted," and Morris, because of his shock of hair, "Topsy." The world went very well in those days with this Oxford brotherhood.

Black mantle bottle green silk dress, black bands. pink roses black lace on bonnet.

black bonnet trimmed green.

FIG. 4.—" Le Journal des Modes " (1853).

The friends do not seem to have been very much affected by the troubles of the times. The Crimean War was waged between 1854–56, and, like all wars, was waged badly. The noble work of Florence Nightingale, however, can be said to have started modern nursing. The ineptitude of the Crimean War was followed by the horrors of the Indian Mutiny. It was a war scare in the winter of 1859–60 which led to the formation of the Volunteers. Morris became one and duly went to camp on Wimbledon Common. The Volunteers much later on were to be transformed by Lord Haldane into the Territorial Army.

On the other hand, men were working away quietly at scientific pursuits which were to effect great alterations in everyday life and things. It was in 1857 that Pasteur submitted the paper to the Lille Scientific Society which was the beginning of his great work on fermentation. If this was caused by minute living organisms, then the possibilities of Pasteur's discovery were endless, and we shall see in the chapter on Public Health how they were realized.

In 1858 the first of the cables to America was laid, but the rejoicings were dashed on its failure after only a few weeks' working, and the communication was not restored until the *Great Eastern* safely laid the next cable in 1866.

Again, in 1859 Darwin was to publish " The Origin of the Species " and turn men's ideas to evolutionary processes. Science was stimulated, and men sought to elucidate the mysteries ; life became fuller and richer.

Street moved his office to London in the autumn of 1856, and Morris went with him, but gave up architecture at the end of the year. Burne-Jones had already gone to London and was studying painting under the guidance of Rossetti, who introduced him to Madox-Brown and Holman Hunt.

Holman Hunt's " Light of the World " had been exhibited at the Royal Academy in 1854, and so that the pre-Raphaelites should not have it all their own way there was as well a landscape group of the Royal Family in Highland costume, and Maclise's " Marriage of Strongbow and Eva." Holman Hunt's " Scapegoat " and Frith's " Derby Day " date from the Royal Academy of 1856. Burne-Jones got into touch with Rossetti through the Working Men's College, in Great Ormond Street, London, founded by Denison Maurice, where University men lectured on science and history, and Rossetti taught drawing.

Morris now fell under the influence of Rossetti, who was a very dominant personality, and he too began painting. In 1857 he and Burne-Jones moved to the first floor of 17 Red Lion Square, Holborn, London, and if any of our readers care to go there they can see the centre window which gave additional light for the painting of the friends.

It was the furnishing of these rooms which started Morris off in his life's work. Remember there was practically nothing to be bought ready-made which Burne-Jones or Morris would have cared to live with. This

Girl's white bonnet, black lace, blue ribbons.
black silk coat, silk ruching, white sleeves,
blue and white plaid silk dress white stockings.
Boy's grey cloth tunic trimmed brown. white
shirt, striped socks, white feather.

FIG. 5.—" Les Modes Parisiennes " (1855).

does not mean that the ordinary furniture of the period was shoddy, machine-made stuff. On the contrary, it was well made by hand, but hideous. Curiously enough, antiques had not yet come into their own, and were thought of as old-fashioned. The Madox-Brown family got over one difficulty by using on their own table the common English willow pattern plates which were generally used in the kitchen.

We have already illustrated in Vol. III some of the horrors of the furnishings which were exhibited at the 1851 Exhibition, and these were the best of the worst. Pugin had exhibited furniture, but it was too ecclesiastical for domestic use and too much in the taste of the Gothic Revival. This is a point to be noted here, that, though Morris was Goth rather than Greek, he was not by any means a medievalist, a revivalist, or restorer—he wished to carry on the Gothic tradition. In the furnishing of the rooms at Red Lion Square, Morris and Burne-Jones were assisted by their friend Webb, who was still with Street.

The next momentous step was when Morris fell in love with Jane Burden in 1857, and, marrying her, in 1859 set up housekeeping at 41 Great Ormond Street, London. But this was only regarded as a temporary measure, and the friends started hunting for a site on which a house could be built worthy of Morris' beautiful bride. This was eventually found at Upton, Bexley, Kent, and Webb left Street's office to design the building. It is interesting to note here that his successor with Street was Norman Shaw, of whom we shall have more to say later on.

This house, which Webb designed and Morris built, was to be of the greatest interest and importance, and the Webb enthusiast likes to refer to it as the very first of the Red Houses which after this were to become a common, almost too common, feature of the countryside. We are not quite so sure ourselves that it should be hailed as the very beginning ; George Devey was another architect who about this time, or even a little earlier, was designing houses which were very good indeed—we shall illustrate one later. His work, however, had not the importance of Webb's, done as this was in conjunction with men like Morris, Jones and Rossetti. Their power came in that they worked as a group.

We deal with Red House later—sufficient to say here that the work which Morris and Jones began in furnishing their bachelor quarters in Red Lion Square was continued with greater enthusiasm now that there was a Mrs. Morris to help.

1860–1869

Out of this work came the firm of Messrs. Morris, Marshall, Faulkner & Co. Marshall was a friend of Madox-Brown's. Faulkner, an old Oxford friend, and then a civil engineer in London, looked after the business side and was a general handyman. Burne-Jones and Madox-Brown made designs for stained glass. Webb designed furniture, and Powell's of White-friars blew glass from his designs. Albert Moore and William de Morgan helped on occasion, and so did Rossetti. When wallpapers were started these were print-ed by Messrs. Jeffreys. Prem-ises were taken in 1861 at 8, Red Lion Square, and they called them-selves "Fine Art *Workmen* in Paint-ing, Carving, Fur-niture, and the Metals."

bodice laced at back, skirt, large double pleats.

cream silk dress flower patterned green ruching lace flounce.

FIG. 6.—London Museum (1860).

This is an important detail—they seem to have gone into business just like good tradesmen. There was nothing precious about them, and they were out, as good workmen, to make good things at a reasonable price. There was no greenery-yallery affectation about them. The first work seems to have been mainly in the direction of decorating churches, and Street and Bodley employed them. Their motto seems to have been, "Have nothing in your houses that you do not know to be useful or believe to be beauti-ful." The architecture of the period can be judged by the Law Courts, London, the competition for which was won by George Edmund Street (1824–81) in 1867, or the Albert

Memorial of George Gilbert Scott (1811–78) of 1864. He it was who did St. Pancras Station and Hotel, in 1865. With the death of the Prince Consort in 1861 one of the makers of modern England passed on.

While our friends were peacefully making furniture the fate of the English-speaking peoples was being decided on the other side of the Atlantic. Slavery or its abolition had come to the forefront as the most important issue in America. The great Abraham Lincoln was to say, " A house divided against itself cannot stand. I believe this Government cannot endure permanently half slave and half free. I do not expect the Union to be dissolved—I do not expect the house to fall—but I do expect it will cease to be divided. It will become all one thing, or all the other." Fortunately for the world it became all free, but one immediate effect was that while the Southern States were fighting they could not grow cotton, and so supplies were cut off from the English cotton mills, with great hardship to masters and men in Lancashire.

Another point to remember is that the Civil War first put ironclads into action, and so started the long course of all-steel battleship construction. The Southern Confederates raised the Northern Federal *Merrimac*, and sheathed her sides with iron plates and renamed her the *Virginia*. The Northern *Monitor* had a long, low body with an iron-plated revolving turret, with two guns inside, and this was called derisively either a " tin can on a shingle," or a " cheesebox on a raft."

Then emigration was continuing—there is Ford Madox Brown's (1821–93) picture in the Tate, the " Last of England " (Fig. 152a) as a reminder—so there was not a home in England, or for that matter in the north of Europe, that was not deeply concerned in the welfare of America and the way she solved her problems, and half the country was still to be settled. When Lincoln was elected President in 1860 the U.S.A. consisted of the territory east of and including Minnesota, Iowa, Missouri, Arkansas and Louisiana, and west of this there was only Oregon, California and Texas. Nearly half the country was not settled and did not vote.

To return to England. By 1865 Morris had become so busy that he was unable to continue to live at Red House. Professor Mackail writes movingly in his "Life of Morris" of the life led by Morris at Red House. It must have been one of the happiest periods in his life, and one of the most interesting groups of men who have ever been drawn together.

FIG. 7.—Croquet (1861).

So Morris had to leave Red House, with its garden and bowling green, and transport himself and family to live over and in his shop at 26 Queen Square, Bloomsbury, the Red Lion Square workshops being given up. He was beginning to burn the candle at both ends.

In 1867 the firm decorated the Green Dining-room at the Victoria and Albert Museum at South Kensington. As it remains to-day in good condition it is proof that Morris & Co. were very honest workmen using good materials. This room should be visited.

The publication of Ruskin's "Unto This Last" (which appeared first in parts in the *Cornhill Magazine*) in 1862 was to point out once more one's duty to one's neighbour, and,

beaver hat
black feather
red neck
ribbon.

black cloth dress
trimmed black
braid and ball
fringe.
white collar.
and cuffs.

FIG. 8.—Riding Habit, "Le Journal des Demoiselles" (1863).

as we shall see, it made a great impression on the mind of Morris. William Booth commenced his work in the East End of London, and the Salvation Army came into being in the early summer of 1865 and preached the Gospel to the "down and outs."

Then in 1866, after several attempts, a cable was laid to America, which vastly improved the communication between the English-speaking races.

Other happenings of this period were: first, the London sewerage system of 1864; second, the application of Pasteur's principles to surgery in 1867 by Joseph Lister, a young surgeon in Glasgow. These improved the health of the people. Of this great man, Joseph Lister, we shall have more to say later; sufficient here to note that the immediate result of his work, together with the use of chloroform as an anæsthetic, was to reduce human suffering and mortality.

Here is a note calculated to make the collector grind his teeth yet give the young poet hope. About 1861 Swinburne bought a first edition of Fitzgerald's "Omar Khayyám" for 1*d*. This, published in 1859 by Quaritch, had been a dead failure, so it was placed outside a shop in a bargain box. Again Ruskin was living at Denmark Hill, which was still a pleasant part of London, and Whistler, who was to deal the group a mortal blow, was meeting them at a party at Madox-Brown's in 1865. Legros was another friend.

It was about this time that the group, which had inherited the traditions of the Pre-Raphaelites, strengthened itself by recruits, and so had influence in other directions. One of Lady Burne-Jones' sisters married John Lockwood Kipling

FIG. 9.—Archery (1870).

and had a son, called Rudyard, because that was the place where his parents met, and another sister married Alfred Baldwin, from whom Stanley Baldwin is descended. It will not be an impertinence to trace the present Conservative chief's happy turn of phrase and literary leanings to his early upbringing and surroundings.

Another immortal happening in this decade was the publication of " Alice's Adventures in Wonderland " in

13

FIG. 10.—Riding Habit (1871).

1866. "Through the Looking-Glass, and What Alice found There," came out in 1872. We have recently had the pleasure of introducing these tales to a young gentleman aged four, and to our joy he enjoyed them just as much as we did when young; in fact, he borrowed an idea from the White Knight and took a mouse-trap out in the car, because "if they *do* come, I don't choose to have them running all about."

1870–79

The decade opened badly with the war between France and Prussia, and readers of Vallery-Radot's "Life of Pasteur" can judge of its unhappy effects on the lives of the peoples, and the enmities of which we still bear the burden. One extraordinary thing was that, though our Lister had applied Pasteur's discoveries to surgery in 1867, the French surgeons did not follow his example in the first battles, so that the condition of the wounded then was not much better than it had been in the Crimea.

The Education Act of 1870 provided that all children should be compelled to receive an elementary education. This does not mean that the schools built as a result were the first elementary schools. The National Society for Promoting the Education of the Children of the Poor in

Fig. 11.—Manor House, Kelmscott. Drawn by E. H. New. An illustration from the "Life of William Morris," by J. W. Mackail, published by Longmans Green & Co., Ltd.

the Principles of the Established Church had begun its good work as early as 1811. Education was much to the fore at this time. Women especially had been agitating for some years that the education of girls should be placed on as favourable a basis as that of boys. Bedford College, London, had been founded in 1849. This was followed by Cheltenham College for Girls in 1854, and then in the 'seventies the movement gained fresh impetus. The Girls' Public Day Schools Co., and Girton College, Cambridge, were founded in 1872, and Newnham in 1875. Perhaps the most momentous happening was that the London School of Medicine for Women opened its doors to students in 1874. At the same time meetings were being held in favour of women's suffrage.

It was in 1871 that Morris bought the Manor House at Kelmscott, near Lechlade, and shared it with Rossetti. This lovely old house was to be a great solace to the friends. Here Morris was able to retire when the business became too much for him and go fishing. By the courtesy of

Brown costume
trimmed
blue silk

brown hat.
blue ribbons
brown feathers..

fur
muff

FIG. 12.—" The Milliner and Dressmaker "
(1871).

Messrs. Longmans, Green & Co., the publishers of the "Life of William Morris," by J. W. Mackail, we are allowed to publish here one of Mr. E. H. New's delightful drawings which illustrate the book (Fig. 11). Kelmscott was to be an abiding love with Morris, and his other houses, and last of all his press, were named after it. In 1873 William Morris left Queen Square to live at Hammersmith—the business seems to have continually encroached on Morris' living quarters, until he had to go.

It was about 1874 that experiments began to be made with dyes. The old vegetable dyes, indigo, woad, madder, and weld for yellow, had been forgotten, and aniline dyes had taken their place. So Morris plunged into experiments and the dye vats in so doing. Here he showed his wisdom, because he conducted these experiments with the assistance of Thomas Wardle of Leek, a well-known dyer. He never seems to have started designing until he had mastered the practical details of the craft, etc. At this period Morris startled his friends by hands and arms blue to the elbow by dabbling in indigo. The first yarns he dyed

16

seem to have been used for carpets. Some of the old partners seceded about this time, and the firm became Morris & Co. in 1875.

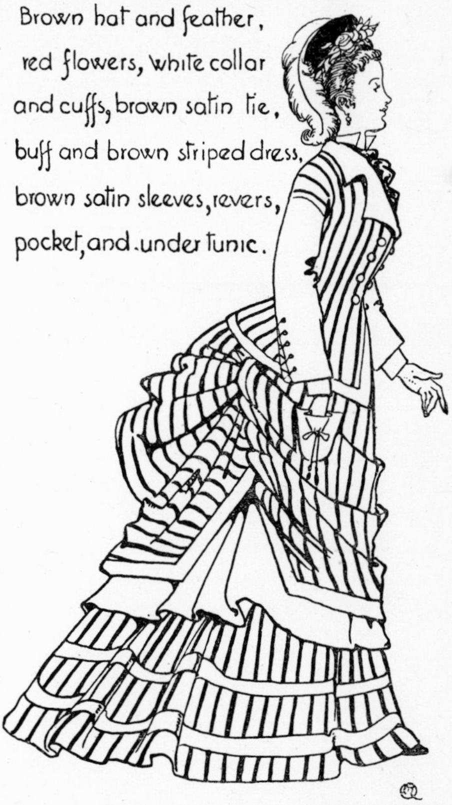

Now we come to a very interesting period of Morris' life, which marks first his introduction to public life, and secondly shows how far ahead he was of his own time. Terrible things were being done about this time in the way of what was called "Restoration," and these things were being done by the parsons and architects. The parsons, especially if they were keen, wished their churches to be as Gothic as possible, so they were apt to call in the architects and try and restore their appearance to what they imagined they had been in pre-Reformation times. Perfectly genuine Renaissance work was thrown out and mock "Gothic" stuff put in its place, all freshly varnished from the church furnishing firms.

Brown hat and feather, red flowers, white collar and cuffs, brown satin tie, buff and brown striped dress, brown satin sleeves, revers, pocket, and under tunic.

FIG. 13.—"Le Journal des Modes" (1875).

The classic case of *restoration* occurred when Butterfield, as a leading Gothicist and the architect of Keble College, Oxford, was called in, about 1870, to restore Winchester College Chapel. Wren was working there about 1684, and it must have been then that he introduced a very lovely oak screen, wall panelling, and altar rails. The screen had perforated panels, in the manner of the staircase at Guildford we illustrated in Fig. 81, Vol. II. Manners makyth man, but neither the College authorities nor Butterfield had any architectural manners, so Wren's panelling was ripped out and sold for an old song. It was not "Gothic"— that was enough. But we can hardly point a finger of scorn at these people, because only recently we have wantonly destroyed, in Waterloo Bridge, one of the world's great bridges. It is a classic example of Bumbledom's stupidity, which has led to no gain.

It was about 1877 that Sir Gilbert Scott was contemplating an onslaught on Tewkesbury Abbey, and Morris rushed into the fray. He wrote to the *Athenæum*, pointing out that old buildings were of historical importance; that when in the thirteenth century they wished to alter or add to a Norman building they did not do it in sham Norman, but in work of their own period, and that so it had remained down through the ages, with the result that the building could be read almost like a document. To attempt to "restore" a building was to attempt the impossible—he pleaded for reparation so that the fabric should be maintained, and attacked the restorers. This led to the formation of the Society for the Protection of Ancient Buildings in 1877, and Morris was its first secretary. Carlyle was a member of what became known as the "Anti-Scrape," and but for the work which it did then, and since, there would hardly be an old building, recognizable as such, left to us now.

Another happening of architectural importance was the designing of St. Agnes' Church, Kennington, in 1875, by George Gilbert Scott, jun., the son of Sir Gilbert.

So far as Morris' own work was concerned, dyeing, calico printing and weaving were much to the fore now, and a new show-room was opened in Oxford Street, opposite to where Selfridge's now is. In 1878 Morris added lecturing on the Decorative Arts to his other activities and

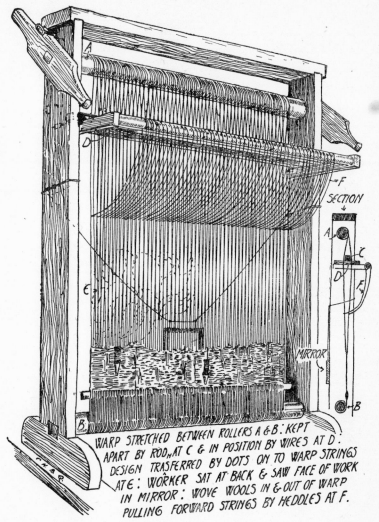

WARP STRETCHED BETWEEN ROLLERS A & B : KEPT
APART BY ROD, AT C & IN POSITION BY WIRES AT D :
DESIGN TRASFERRED BY DOTS ON TO WARP STRINGS
AT E : WORKER SAT AT BACK & SAW FACE OF WORK
IN MIRROR : WOVE WOOLS IN & OUT OF WARP
PULLING FORWARD STRINGS BY HEDDLES AT F.

FIG. 14.—Model of Morris' Tapestry Loom.
(*Victoria and Albert Museum.*)

moved to another house in the Upper Mall, Hammersmith,
where he was to pass the rest of his days, and he altered
the name of this to Kelmscott House, showing how he
loved the other Kelmscott. Here it was that he had a
tapestry loom put up in his bedroom so that he could work
at it if he happened to wake early. This was typical of the

FIG. 15.—Roller Skating (1875).

man—he wished to revive the art of high-warp tapestry weaving. He looked ahead and realized that, with Burne-Jones to help, fine work could be done—so he experimented himself until he understood the medium.

Figure 14 shows Morris' high-warp tapestry loom, and it is interesting to note that he has gone back to a type of which we saw the beginning in our book on " Homeric Greece." In Fig. 40 there Penelope is shown weaving the shroud for Laertes on a high-warp loom. Carpet looms were installed in the converted stables of the house as Fig. 16—hence the beautiful Hammersmith carpets. This year, however (1878) was a bad year, because Morris, who was overtaxing his strength, contracted rheumatic gout, and the group was to be challenged.

In 1878 the *Whistler* v. *Ruskin* action was heard in the Law Courts, and this was of the greatest importance, because it was far more than a quarrel between two men ; it was a fight between two schools. Pre-Raphaelism had

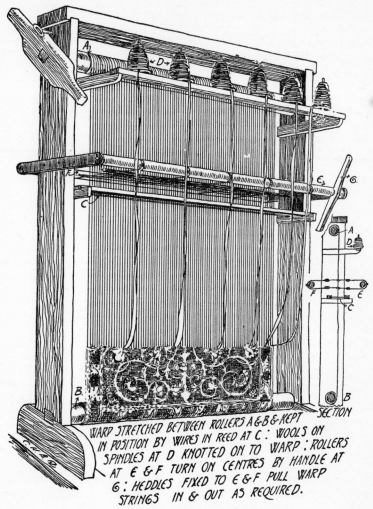

WARP STRETCHED BETWEEN ROLLERS A & B & KEPT
IN POSITION BY WIRES IN REED AT C : WOOLS ON
SPINDLES AT D KNOTTED ON TO WARP : ROLLERS
AT E & F TURN ON CENTRES BY HANDLE AT
G : HEDDLES FIXED TO E & F PULL WARP
STRINGS IN & OUT AS REQUIRED.

FIG. 16.—Model of Morris' Carpet Loom.
(*Victoria and Albert Museum.*)

expended its vigour, and Impressionism was knocking at
the door. Whistler (1834–1903) had exhibited at the
newly founded Grosvenor Gallery in 1877, and took
umbrage at a criticism by Ruskin which he considered was
damaging to his reputation. Whistler was a peppery individual so he struck at Ruskin as the High Priest of Pre-
Raphaelism. The action turned on good workmanship.

Olive green cloth dress.
brown silk frills
brown silk braid and
embroidery and bow.

FIG. 17.—" Le Journal des Modes " (1875).

Burne-Jones gave evidence on Ruskin's behalf, and said that he thought perfect finish was necessary. In his judgment " The Nocturne in Blue and Silver " was "an incomplete work of art," and Battersea Bridge was " formless." "The Nocturne in Black and Gold " he did not think could be ranked as a work of art at all. A Titian was produced in court as an illustration of finish. The lawyers thoroughly enjoyed themselves, and in the end Whistler got $\frac{1}{4}d$. damages and no costs. As the " Nocturne in Blue and Silver " and the " Nocturne in Black and Gold," with the " Symphony in White, No. 2," are now at the National Gallery, and " Old Battersea Bridge " and two fine portraits are now at the Tate, our readers can go and see the pictures and judge for themselves. While at the National see as well the " Firing Party," by Edouard Manet (1832–83), in the Impressionist School, and the fifteenth-century John van Eyck of " Jan Arnolfini and his Wife," which Burne-Jones thought one of the great pictures of the world—here is " finish " if you like.

The Grosvenor Gallery, where Whistler had exhibited the work which offended Ruskin, was to be satirized by Gilbert in "Patience," first produced in 1881. "Greenery yallery, Grosvenor Gallery, foot in the grave young man" poked good fun at the æsthete of the day. Whistler was to go to law again in 1895 with Sir William Eden about the painting of Lady Eden. This case led to the publication of "The Baronet and the Butterfly."

Green bonnet, white feather, green cloth dress, green satin band, bow and sash, kilted cloth frills. Over tunic and cuffs of green brocade

FIG. 18.—"Le Journal des Modes" (1878)

Other interesting happenings in this decade were: The appointment of Ruskin as Slade Professor at Oxford in 1870, which extended his influence and led to him making his undergraduates build roads in 1874. The Suez Canal was opened in 1872, and shortened the voyage to India. Telephones were installed in London in 1876 and speeded up business, and in 1880 the first cargo of frozen beef reached us from Australia. All these things were to be revolutionary in the sense that they were destined to alter our mode of living.

1880–89

In 1881 Morris & Co. moved to Merton Abbey, where it

was that tapestry was really begun. The technical difficulties of reviving this ancient craft must have been enormous, but Figs. 70 and 87 show how well they were overcome. It was in 1882 that Morris cast in his lot with the Socialists. As we are said to be all Socialists now, it will be well to try and go back in imagination and find out why certain people were moved in this direction, and why others opposed them. If we could go right back to Weston in the eighteenth century, when Parson Woodforde was there, of whom we wrote in Vol. III, we should find a small community in which all the people knew one another, and where public opinion was very strong. The lazy, cruel and oppressive people were very soon found out, and had to amend their ways or be pilloried by public opinion, and the poor were helped by the charitable. This was not possible in the early nineteenth century, when the large industrial towns were becoming "Wens," as Cobbett called them. It was nobody's business to lend a helping hand to the less fortunate. The master could not know all his men, and when the mill gates closed he was done with them and they went home to their back-to-back houses, and no account was taken of public health. We do not suggest that the early nineteenth century folk were more cruel than their ancestors. They honestly believed in a surplus of cheap labour which would help them to develop industry, and that surplus was being provided by the agricultural labourer, who was coming into the towns to seek work. Agricultural depression was being caused by the ever-increasing importation of foreign corn and the beginnings of the frozen meat trade (see Chapter II). It was nobody's business to look for trouble, so nobody did, and matters went from bad to worse. Then men began to arise who said that such a state of affairs must be remedied. Robert Owen at the beginning of the century had made a beginning in looking after the living, as well as the dead machinery, and he was followed by many others.

24

Ruskin's "Unto this Last," which first appeared in parts in the *Cornhill Magazine,* was published in book form in 1862, and seems to have influenced Morris and his group. Read to-day it is the mildest reminder that working for profit is not the final end and aim of existence. What we have to remember is that it really was considered to be so.

Ruskin declared that this was not the case and instanced various types of men who did not always act for selfish interest. Though he did not use the example, we

Straw hat pink roses peacock ribbons.

Cream voile dress, peacock blue ribbons lace at neck and sleeves.

FIG. 19.—"Myra's Journal" (1884).

can. Pasteur, of whom we shall be writing later, excited the interest and curiosity of Napoleon III and the Empress Eugenie, and explained the work he was doing on fermentation to them. They expressed wonder that he should not take steps to protect his interests and make money by his discoveries. Pasteur, a man of the noblest character, told them as kindly as he could that no man can serve two masters.

To return to Architecture. Norman Shaw, who followed Philip Webb as head assistant to Street, started practice in 1862, and very soon became the leading architect of the day. He it was who was responsible, about

1880, for the development of Bedford Park, London, which must be noted here as one of the first attempts to produce something on Garden City lines.

The Boys' Brigade was founded in 1883 ; it has a world strength of over 120,000, with an object defined as " the Advancement of Christ's Kingdom among Boys." Drill is successfully used for discipline, but the movement is in no sense militaristic. The curriculum includes a wide range of such subjects as Physical Training, Camping, Swimming, and Games. There are 2,700 Companies in the United Kingdom (1,700 in England), and each is connected with a Church or Chapel. In 1884 Toynbee Hall was founded in the East End of London to bring rich and poor together, and in the same year the Fabian Society was formed by men like Sidney Webb and Bernard Shaw.

In 1884 the Art Workers' Guild was founded. Morris, Walter Crane, T. J. Cobden-Sanderson, Heywood Sumner, W. R. Lethaby and W. A. S. Benson were original members. The same group, with Benson as the leader, founded the Arts and Crafts Society in 1887, and in this year Bellamy published " Looking Backward."

The Arts and Crafts Movement was largely a reflection of the Socialistic group. Again another opportunity was missed ; all this energy should have gone into more ordinary channels. But a clean cut was made ; it was felt to be more honest to learn to weave or make furniture than gamble on the Stock Exchange. Benson, however, who was an architect, started a shop in Bond Street and sold metal-work which was very good indeed.

It was an era of Social Reform and University Settlements. Morris, with his enormous energy, threw himself into the cause, and preached at street corners and addressed meetings all over the place. Burne-Jones could not follow him here, and it was the one thing the friends did not share. Morris went to breakfast on Sunday mornings with Burne-Jones, and then left after to do his Socialistic work and preach the Gospel as he interpreted it. Morris was dominated by Socialism till about 1886, and then, though still working hard in the cause, he turned back to his own work. In 1888 he became friendly with Emery Walker, and so became interested in typography. This led up to the work of the Kelmscott Press.

People found time, however, to amuse themselves very well in the eighties. Gilbert and Sullivan, who had begun their wonderful partnership in light opera with " Trial by Jury " in 1875, continued nearly each year to bring out another classic until

White figured silk dress, lace overskirt.

tulle chemisette

Humming birds, and pearl trimming.

FIG. 20.—" Le Journal des Modes " (1885).

" Utopia " in 1893. At the Gaiety there were Terry, Nellie Farren, and Kate Vaughan, on whom old gentlemen still wax lyrical.

While all this was going on two things were to happen of tremendous importance. The first was the discovery of gold on the Rand in 1884, which was to bring Johannesburg into being and begin the grab for Africa. From the days of the Argonauts, gold has always brought trouble in its train, and it was so in South Africa. The Boers, who had thought themselves secure from intrusion since they trekked to the Transvaal, now found their country pervaded by a set of people far removed from the pastoral life; they concentrated on the large-scale extraction of gold. A clash was inevitable anyhow, and the trouble came with the futile Jameson Raid of 1896, which was followed by the South African War of 1899–1903. But the breach was later healed (*v.* p. 37) and South Africa is working manfully in the Empire's war effort.

The other important happening was that Daimler invented a light high-speed spirit motor, or engine, and then Carl Benz applied such a motor to a vehicle, and so built the first motor-car, in 1885. Speed on land now became possible, and speed at sea was improved by the steam turbine which Parsons invented in 1884.

Another political happening was the Home Rule Bill for Ireland of 1886. The crossing of Greenland by Nansen in 1888 gave boys a taste for adventure, and Kipling published his "Plain Tales from the Hills" in 1888.

In 1887 came the Queen's Jubilee. She had reigned fifty years, and since the death of the Prince Consort had withdrawn herself—but now came the time of rejoicing. One of the authors can remember being taken to Green Park, at the bottom of Constitution Hill, looking across the entrance to the Palace. Hours passed by, during which the guests arrived and the procession was marshalled, and then the hour itself came when the Queen set out. In Athens in the old days, every fourth year the people went in procession to the Acropolis, bearing with them on the yard of a ship a new robe for Athene. In London in 1887 it was almost as if Athene herself processed before her people, accompanied by her soldiers and sailors and all the peoples from over the seas—a very rare show indeed.

But the decade was to finish with a stern reminder that it was no good talking of Social Reform—something must be done. In the great Dock Strike of 1889 the dockers struck for the "docker's tanner," or 6*d.* an hour, and John Burns came to the fore as their leader. It was more soul-stirring than the Jubilee; people were shocked at such a state of affairs. And they could no longer plead ignorance, because Charles Booth's monumental survey of the "Life and Labour of the People in London" came out, in seventeen volumes, between 1889–1902. Here were all the facts of the life of the poor.

In 1889 the Arts and Crafts Society held an exhibition, and Morris gave a lecture on Gothic Architecture.

1890–99

The beginning of the decade is memorable for the Act of 1891, which made elementary education not only compulsory, but free, and this has gradually developed until to-day many children are now fed in addition, and all are medically examined, and some treated.

It was about this time that Morris asked Emery Walker to be partners with him in a printing scheme. Typography, or the art of the printed page,

FIG. 21.—Golf Clothes (1889)

was at a very low ebb, except for the work of a few men like Walker, who were doing their best to improve matters. Morris wanted to turn out gloriously decorated books, and in this he was helped by Walker, who, without becoming a business partner, gave advice as a friend, and Burne-Jones did many of the decorations, and so the Kelmscott Press came into being. In 1890 the new type was being prepared, and Morris took the greatest care over this. Producing good type is a matter of the greatest difficulty. The first essential is that it should produce printing which is clear to read and good to look at. Printing was begun in 1891, and the first book printed was "The Story of

29

the Glittering Plain." In 1892 came Ruskin's "On the Nature of Gothic," from the "Stones of Venice," and in the preface Morris stated the effect which this book had had on his life and work. The great Kelmscott "Chaucer" was his last work, and he died on October 3rd, 1896, aged sixty-three, through having attempted to do the work of seven men, and with him an epoch was closed.

Professor Mackail gives a delightful letter from Morris to Webb dated August 27th, 1894. Morris had been sending Webb Kelmscott Press books as they appeared, and Webb had evidently remonstrated with him at the extent of his generosity. So Morris' letter, which began "My dear Fellow" and ended "Yours affectionately," told the tale of a traveller in America who entered an inn and ordered chicken for his dinner. The clerk who received the order answered by taking out a revolver and, after covering the guest, remarked, "Stranger, you will not have chicken, you will have hash"—so Webb was to have the Kelmscott books as they came out, whether he liked or no. This friendship was a very beautiful thing.

There can be no doubt that it was the astounding vigour of Morris which animated the group. Without him the Arts and Crafts Movement faded out of the picture to have a renaissance a little later on the Continent. People were no longer interested in "tracing out this grey, shadowy, many-pinnacled image of the Gothic spirit within us ; and discerning what fellowship there is between it and our Northern hearts"—so Beowulf and Arthur and the heroes of the "Burnt Njal Saga" retired into the shadows once more and the people turned to the modern world. Burne-Jones died in 1898, and Webb seems to have been disheartened, because he retired in 1900.

"Three Houses," by Angela Thirkell, is very interesting, because it gives an account of the Burne-Jones and Morris family group from the grand-daughter's point of view. One thing Mrs. Thirkell notices is the absence of any real comfort in her grandparents' three houses. They sat

straight-backed in their rush-bottomed chairs while talking of their
heroes.

Life was becoming safer.
Pasteur and Lister had shown
how the microbe could be slain ;
the public health was much
better. Ronald Ross was to
discover in 1897 that the malarial
parasite was carried by the mosquito, and this enabled the white
man to carry on his work safely
in regions where before he had
not been able to go.

Then speed began to be
thought of. The machine
was more used—if the profits
were smaller, the returns were
quicker. Henry Ford was to
build his first car in 1893, and
his ideal was not to provide the
rich man with a plaything, but
the populace with cheap transport ; in doing this he invented

FIG. 22.—Cricket Dress
(1890).

Mass Production. Even England realized the possibilities.
Benz produced his first car in 1885, but it could not be
used in England because of the law of 1865, which required
all mechanically propelled vehicles not to exceed four miles
an hour, and two miles in towns, and to be preceded by
a man carrying a red flag—his rate settled that of the
vehicle. The Act of 1896 gave the red-flag man the sack
and allowed a speed of twelve miles per hour.

This was to revolutionize transport, and still later,
as work became more mechanical, and men's lives
consequently less interesting, they were to seek relief in
dashing about at high speed, until to-day the roads,
some of which were first laid down by the Romans, have

become racing tracks on which the lives of men, women and children are daily sacrificed. A beginning, however, was made in taking traffic off the roads in 1890, when the City and South London Railway was opened. This was the first electrically operated railway in Great Britain, and the first Tube in the world.

As if all this was not enough, Burne-Jones read one night in bed of " a clever young chap " at Bologna University, twenty-two years old, called Marconi, who had invented a little machine about the size of a sewing machine, and with it could communicate with anyone having a similar machine, and there were no wires in between ; in fact, it was Wireless.

The rejoicings of the 1887 Jubilee were renewed and redoubled in those of the 1897 Diamond Jubilee. The country was at peace, and the ordinary people did not attach very much importance to the Jameson Raid of 1896, or the Fashoda incident, which nearly caused war between England and France.

By 1888 Norman Shaw was designing 170 Queen's Gate, (Figs. 91 and 92), and had arrived at the Later Renaissance, or real " Queen Anne." We discuss all this later and in more detail, and a special study of the life and work and pupils of Norman Shaw has been written by Sir Reginald Blomfield, R.A., and issued in 1940 by our publishers.

But if all this showed that man was marching with the times and accustoming himself to big business, making money and being very civilized and Greek, there remained the other side of him, which liked the country and was Gothic. So into the country he went for the week-ends and built a house for himself. If he had made sufficient money it was surrounded by a park and had a lodge, and there might be a farmery with some Jersey cows. Old houses began to be sought out and restored, and the agents advertised them as being full of old oak beams ; or new ones were built, and the more gabled the roofs and lead glazed the windows the better. Then golf was brought down from the North, because it was a real Gothic game, and one which called for good whiskery, rustic clothes, and after 1896 a car could be bought, to give the final touch of incongruity to a country life which was about as real as that of Marie Antoinette. The first number of *Country Life Illustrated* appeared on January 8th, 1897. It made known all the old houses to the townsman, and tried to teach him country manners.

White silk dress, spotted tulle

Red velvet bows and streamers

pleated panels.

FIG. 23.—"Le Journal des Modes" (1894).

If all this was a little unreal, other things were happening which were more important. The period is memorable for the publication in 1898 of " To-morrow," by Ebenezer Howard, which seems to have been inspired by Bellamy's " Looking Backward." As we shall see on p. 83, the beginning of the modern town-planning movement in England dates from the publication of " To-morrow."

The Franco-German War was well behind in the memories of middle-aged people, and the Crimea forgotten. Then clouds began to appear on the South African horizon and the rejoicings of the Jubilee were quenched by the disasters of the South African War. What was worse, the sympathies of our neighbours seemed to be with our opponents, and it almost looked as if we might be driven into the sea instead of the Boers. Volunteers were called for, and " dukes' sons, cooks' sons, and the sons of belted earls " went out to save us from defeat. So the old Queen's reign finished in gloom.

1900–14

In this period the new century opened. People were full of hope—would the new century be better than the old and the pursuit of happiness more possible. The long reign of Victoria had been memorable for many things. When the young Queen had come to the throne in 1837 the rather grubby doings of the Regent and his brothers had been forgotten in a period which prided itself on its respectability, and money had been made by the frugal manufacturers and merchants. When the old Queen died, who had reigned so wisely and well, and Edward, who was held to be a " good sort," came to the throne it was felt that the time had come to spend the money. The merchants' sons went to expensive preparatory schools and public schools, and the best colleges in the older universities, and frugality was not a subject to which much attention was given. Life became gayer.

Yet things were happening which were to smash this life to smithereens. In 1900 Germany passed a Navy Law which showed that, having consolidated her successes on land, she was now to challenge us on the sea. In 1903 Joseph Chamberlain began his Tariff Reform League, which in the end was to alter the economic structure of the country and lead to the abandonment of Free Trade and the adoption of Protection once more. Life was speeded up and mechanical vehicles were by the Act of 1903 allowed to move along the roads at twenty miles an hour.

But the most momentous happening in this direction was the first mechanically propelled flight, made by the

34

Wright Brothers in an aeroplane on December 17th, 1903. We saw in Vol. III (Fig. 171) that the people who rode in Trevithicks' " Catch - me - who - can" in 1808 hardly realized its potentialities. Very much the same thing happened with the Wright brothers' first trip by aeroplane. They felt so confident of their success that they sent round invitations to the people in the neighbourhood of Kitty Hawk, North Carolina, to come and see them fly. But there was a nasty cold wind

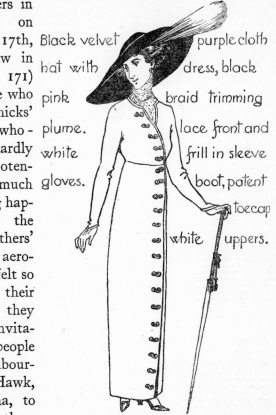

Black velvet hat with pink plume. white gloves.

purple cloth dress, black braid trimming lace front and frill in sleeve boot, patent toecap white uppers.

FIG. 24.—From "Weldon's Ladies' Journal" (1912).

blowing and only five people thought it worth while to turn up. We wonder what the five thought of as the aeroplane rose from the ground and flew for twelve seconds. Did they realize that in a few years Alcock, Whitten Brown, and Lindbergh would fly across the Atlantic; that between 1914 and 1918 and from 1939 onwards men would fight in the air ; and did we realize, when the newspapers began to write of the Wright brothers' achievement, that for the purposes of defence England had ceased to be an island, and navies and warships might be rendered obsolete ?

It must have been a little later than this—perhaps round about 1905—that the authors were walking along Oxford Street, London, on its south side, a little to the east of the Circus, when their attention was attracted to a show that was going on, called Hale's " Tours of the World." A shop front had been taken out, and you were invited to " walk in " and take your places in what looked like a railway coach. Sixpence was charged, and this being paid we took our seats. The guard blew his whistle and waved a flag, and someone made noises like an engine, and the train started, or rather the wheels started and gave us the impression that we were moving. Then at the end of the coach a picture began to flicker, and we found that we were travelling through the countryside of South Africa. It was all magical and mysterious. Another point we remember is that, when the view in front showed that the train was going round a curve, the wheels ground on their flanges in proper style.

This was our introduction to the " pictures," and it was one of the beginnings of entertainment for the masses. In the good old days the working man on a Saturday night went marketing with his missus, and dropped into the " pub," where he might conceivably drink more than was good for him, because there was nowhere else for him to go. With the advent of the pictures the whole family, for a few pence, could see a wonderful spectacle of life. There might not be much artistry about it, but here, on the magic screen, the women were lovely and the men virile, and they lived in splendid surroundings. So they forgot for a moment their own poverty.

The Labour Party was formed in the House of Commons in 1906, and they sought the improvement of the conditions of life for the working classes. One very memorable measure was the introduction by John Burns of the Housing and Town Planning Act of 1909. In this it was suggested that it was a good idea to plan a town before you built it, and that in so doing the amenities should be considered.

SUFFRAGETTES

The Union of the South African States in 1910, with Botha, our late enemy, as the first Prime Minister, was a notable achievement towards peace. At home, however, the politicians raged together, until the Parliament Act of 1911 deprived the House of Lords of the power of rejecting a Money Bill. The Suffragettes demanded the vote, and actually fought for it with tooth and nail. They borrowed an idea from the Siege of Troy, and, concealing themselves in a large removal pantechnicon, drove into Parliament Square and then, descending from their Trojan horse, attempted to rush the doors of the House of Commons. We remember once seeing a line of women among whom were people who might have been one's own wife, sisters, mother or grandmother, marching up Victoria Street until they came to a line of police, who barred their way. The poor policemen looked unhappy as they ran them in, and the only people who were amused were the roughs and toughs. There were troublous times in Ireland, and fighting seemed possible between North and South. Conflict was everywhere.

So events moved forward to the great tragedy of 1914–18. Clearly it is not within our province to attempt to write in detail of this ; and who can ? No Christian parallels are possible. Perhaps Book XX of the Iliad gives us the pagan explanation : " So spake the son of Cronos and roused implacable war. And the gods went forth to the battle, some on this side and some on that."

We pass over the restless unsettled years of the nineteen twenties and thirties with their feverish gaiety, their pre-occupation with social services and swiftly rising taxation, and abroad their earnest but futile efforts at pacts and treaties which should cage the dove of peace. This interlude, as we now know it to be, between the two greatest wars of history, has been recorded pictorially by Cecil Beaton and reviewed by the authors' son Peter, in their book *Time Exposure*.

Then came the menace of German rearmament and

37

Hitler's bid for world conquest, to which the nations of Europe at first were wilfully and tragically blind, and so the stage was set for the greater, sharper, grimmer conflict of 1939 onwards. The power of one ruthless and terribly armed nation, completely disciplined and organized for war, to overrun and subjugate and exploit smaller peoples is, with deadly modern weapons, almost unlimited. The appalling effect of aeroplane bombing has been shown in the destruction wreaked by the R.A.F. on German industrial plants, and more wantonly and indiscriminately on London, Bristol, Plymouth and other cities. Nevertheless, the cities will be rebuilt where they have been wiped out, and many mean and commonplace structures will be replaced by something nobler. But the loss of such treasures as the obliterated Wren churches and their craftsmanship is irreparable, and our deprivation of the fine young lives given gladly in saving Britain from destruction is infinitely greater. Yet peace will return to Europe, and with it the chance to rebuild and reconstruct, though much hard work and sacrificing effort will be needed to effect even a partial restoration, and the idea that an ideal and Utopian state of society will gracefully emerge may be dismissed as a baseless dream ; years and many of them will be required to efface the effects, which will long persist, though in the past humanity, especially the European branch of the race, has shown an amazing quickness and ability in smoothing away the scars and restoring trade and the steady production of industry.

PANEL YELLOW- LETTERING & DECORATIONS IN RED SHADED WITH BLACK

FIG. 25.—Tail-board belonging to Mr. Kiddle, made about 1820.

CHAPTER II

THE FARMER AND FOOD

W E cannot do better than start with the farmer, as we did in Vol. III, because his trade still remains the most important of the three great trades. Man must eat—he can make shift with the skins of animals for clothes, and can find shelter in a cave ; food, however, he must have if he is to survive.

In Vol. III we traced the revolution in agriculture which was effected by the work of Tull and Bakewell. During the eighteenth century agriculture was the greatest industry. The best of the great landlords, like Coke of Holkham, lived on their land and practised farming themselves—it was their job. When Coke entertained his friends at the Holkham gatherings it was a meeting of experts. They would have agreed with the great Dr. Johnson that : " By Agriculture only can commerce be perpetuated ; and by Agriculture alone can we live in plenty without intercourse with other nations. This, therefore, is the great art, which every Government ought to protect, every proprietor of lands to practise, and every inquirer into nature to improve." Coke and his friends probably looked on the people in the rising industrial towns as grubby helots of little importance. Dr. Johnson had pointed out how unstable trade is, how great trading communities had disappeared in the past : " Every trading nation flourishes, while it can be said to flourish, by the courtesy of others. We cannot compel any people to buy from us, or to sell to us." This outlook must be borne in mind.

England was still governed by gentlemen for gentlemen

in the early nineteenth century. The manufacturing interests were not enfranchised until the Reform Bill of 1832 gave the vote to the householder of the £10 a year house. So, after the Napoleonic Wars, the Corn Law of 1815 was passed, which forbade the importation of corn until the price of the home-grown product reached 80s. a quarter. This safeguarded agriculture. It is easy for us, looking back, to condemn this as a very cruel measure. We know by Cobbett that the life of the poor became very hard indeed, but our ancestors could not look forward so easily as we can look back. The time factor must always be borne in mind. Men like Trevithick or the Wright brothers invent a thing, and we wonder that our forebears did not at once realize the possibilities of their inventions— yet years had to pass before this was done. In safeguarding agriculture by the 1815 Corn Laws the statesmen thought they were protecting something of much greater import- ance than Industrialism ; but Industrialism was developing by leaps and bounds. The Corn Law was modified in 1826 by a sliding scale, which admitted colonial corn.

The Industrialists soon began to use the powers which had been conferred on them by the Reform Bill of 1832, and in 1838 an Anti-Corn Law League was founded by Manchester merchants. These people wanted Free Trade, especially in foodstuffs, and they were to be left free to make the very best bargains they could, especially with labour. The artisan did not get the vote until 1867 ; the agricultural labourer until 1884. Cobden, a Lancashire calico printer, and Bright, a Lancashire cotton spinner, were the shining lights and orators of the Anti-Corn Law League, and they conducted meetings all over England for Free Trade. Cobden got into the House of Commons in 1841, and Bright in 1843. Their campaign was helped by the failure of the potato crop in Ireland in 1845, and the terrible distress there, and the difficulty of importing corn led to the total abolition of the Corn Laws in 1846. This date is one of the most important in the history of England.

From then on the Johnsonian doctrine of agriculture being the mother and nurse was forsaken. Manufactured goods were to be exported, and paid for by raw materials and imported foodstuffs. England was to be a workshop, not a farm. Here again we must not condemn the politicians ; this was the position in 1846— there was a chance of catastrophe. Industrialism had expanded to such an extent that it sat in the nest rather like a young cuckoo, and demanded more food than its unfortunate foster-parents were able to provide. There had been a famine in Ireland, and there might well have been one in England as things were before 1846.

FIG. 26.—The Shepherd.

We should like to make a suggestion, and it is that our readers should read " The Mayor of Casterbridge," by Thomas Hardy. This deals with agricultural life in Wessex just before the repeal of the Corn Law. As Hardy writes, " The wheat quotations from month to month depended entirely upon the home harvest. A bad harvest, or the prospect of one, would double the price of corn in a few weeks ; and the promise of a good yield would lower it as rapidly."

So the Harvest Festival in those days was a real

FIG. 27.—Milking.

thanksgiving to God for deliverance from famine. Nowadays, when much of our corn comes from abroad, town child probably regards the service as a pleasant spectacle, and asks its mother what the sheaf is for, and the puzzled mother replies, very quietly, " Wheat, my dear, I think, from which flour is made." The exhibits in a town church should really be in tins.

Read Hardy's books ; they deal with life in Wessex, where agriculture is as old as the long barrows on the hills, and these were built before Stonehenge was erected to observe the rising of the sun on Midsummer Day.

The abolition of the Corn Law in 1846 did not mean that all the farmers were at once ruined. The population was increasing, and there were more mouths to be fed. Wheat was 54s. 8d. a quarter in 1846, 69s. 9d. in 1847, and 50s. 6d. in 1848. In 1849, however, the price declined to 44s. 3d., and there followed lean years until the Crimean War, when 72s. 5d. was realized, and then another decline of prices set in. By 1867 they had improved again to 64s. 5d, and in 1872 57s. was the average price.

To get down to practical details. We are fortunate in having a friend who, born in 1856, has been farming all his life in the Blandford-Wimborne district of Dorset, and we have been allowed to draw on his fund of experience.

FIG. 28.—The Hurdle-maker.

In prices we have been guided as well by " The Record of Seasons' Prices," by T. H. Baker, who farmed up to the 'eighties in the Warminster district.

We will begin with the life led on a Dorset farm of 300 acres about 1872. The rent and tithe paid by the farmer was £600 a year, so land was still a profitable proposition for the landlord. About 200 acres were arable, farmed on the four-course system. This, as we explained in Vol. III, was introduced by Charles Townshend, known as " Turnip " Townshend because of his farming activities carried on about 1730. He planted his fields in the following rotation : First, wheat or oats, sown in the winter; the next year oats or barley, sown in the spring; the third year clover, rye and vetches, and the fourth year turnips, which were eaten off by sheep so that the ground was manured. This system was followed on the 300-acre farm in Dorset. Fifty acres of wheat were grown, 30 acres of barley, and 30 acres of oats. About 200 to 300 lambs were bought in July to August and sold as the roots disappeared.

In addition, forty cows were kept, and these were let to a dairyman at £12 per annum per cow. The contract

FIG. 29.—The Thatcher.

dated from February 14th each year, and the cows were in calf. The calves when they were born were the property of the dairyman, who had as well a good house to live in, and the dairy for his work. The cows remained the farmer's property, and he had to supply good milkers. He also found all the food, with the exception of cake, which the dairyman provided if he thought this advisable. The rent of the cow was about the same as the price of a young cow and calf—£12. The dairyman provided all his own labour, and generally this meant the whole of his family, with some casual help. He sold a little milk, but most of it went into butter and cheese, and he made cheese by the ton and sold it in the local markets or to shops in the country towns. As well he kept pigs.

The farmer was thus assured of an income of £480 per annum from the rent of forty cows let at £12 a cow.

So far as his corn was concerned, he sowed 2 bushels of wheat to the acre on 50 acres, and drilled 10 acres in a day, and if he had a good crop got a return of about 9 sacks, or 36 bushels, to the acre, or a total of 450 sacks

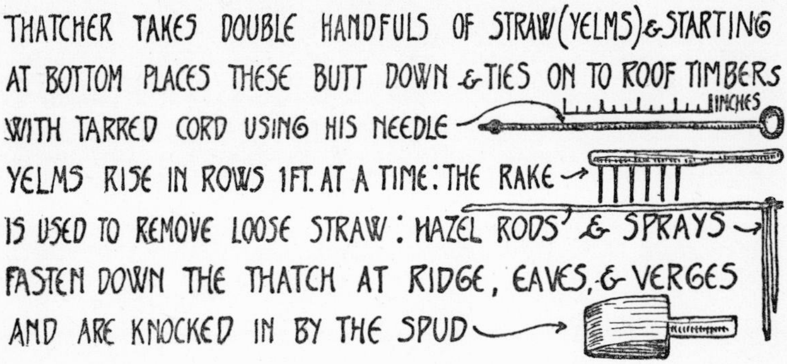

THATCHER TAKES DOUBLE HANDFULS OF STRAW (YELMS) & STARTING
AT BOTTOM PLACES THESE BUTT DOWN & TIES ON TO ROOF TIMBERS
WITH TARRED CORD USING HIS NEEDLE
YELMS RISE IN ROWS 1FT. AT A TIME: THE RAKE
IS USED TO REMOVE LOOSE STRAW: HAZEL RODS & SPRAYS
FASTEN DOWN THE THATCH AT RIDGE, EAVES, & VERGES
AND ARE KNOCKED IN BY THE SPUD

FIG. 30.—The Thatcher's Tools.

on his 50 acres. Two sacks go to the quarter, so if the
Dorset farmer of 1872 sold his wheat at 57s. a quarter,
which as we have seen was the average price for that year,
he obtained £641 for his wheat.

But growing wheat is a gamble ; the season might be
a very bad one and the yield go down to only 19 bushels
the acre. Our farmer on his 300-acre farm was satisfied
if on the average he could sell his wheat for £500, and his
barley for £300. This meant £800 for his corn, plus £480
for the cows, or a total of £1280, and then he hoped to
make £520 a year out of his sheep and any other crops he
could sell, because he aimed at making a total income of
£1800 per annum, or three times his rent of £600. One
£600 went to his landlord, another for his wages and working expenses, and the third for him to live on. If he
could make three times his rent he could thrive, and he
seems to have been able to do so round about 1872. The
countryside was still prosperous.

Now we will turn to the farmer and his establishment
and find out how they lived on this 300-acre farm. There
was the farmer and his two grown-up sons, who all worked
hard, and his wife, who was a good housekeeper and was
assisted by one maid indoors and a groom-gardener to do
odd jobs, and they all lived like fighting cocks on the
freshest and best of plain English food. Tinned stuff and

45

the shrouded corpses of refrigerated animals from the other side of the world did not appear on the farmer's table. Beef and mutton, which had been $6\frac{3}{4}d.$ a pound in 1858, had advanced in 1872 to $8\frac{3}{4}d.$, but pigs produced all the things which a pig does produce, from pork to sausages, hams and bacon, black puddings and chitterlings. Then there were rabbits, hares, pheasants and plump partridges and pigeons. Good fresh milk came from the dairy with cream clotted by scalding to eat with the fruit tarts, and butter and eggs. A good fowl could always be obtained, and a goose for Michaelmas, and turkey for Christmas. The farmer brewed about 10 or 12 hogsheads of cider.

The wheat the farmer grew went to the local water-mill, and there was ground into flour between the millstones. Now here is an interesting point. Growing wheat in our damp climate is always a lottery, and in quality does not make better bread than the wheat imported from Canada. This latter is dryer, and so will take more water and produce more loaves than English wheat. Where the farmer of 1872 scored was that, when he sent his own wheat to the local mill, less was taken out of it than is the case to-day, when everybody wants a white loaf. In the old days the germ (Fig. 49) was left in the flour, and this gave the bread remarkable staying qualities.

As to the price of bread, we have seen that the 1872 Dorset farmer averaged 57s. a quarter for his wheat. At two sacks to the quarter one sack was worth 28s. 6d.; when the farmer sent, say, ten sacks to the miller he received back only seven sacks of flour. The ten sacks of wheat at 250 lb. each = 2500 lb. The seven sacks of flour = 1960 lb., leaving 540 lb. of bran and offals for feeding stuffs, which were the miller's profit. So that ten sacks of wheat at 28s. 6d. each, = £14 5s., had been turned into seven sacks of flour for the same price, or a little over £2 each. This would produce ninety quartern loaves at just over $5\frac{1}{3}d.$ for the quartern. Here is a problem : in this year (1933) we read of bursting granaries and the low

46

price of wheat—yet
the quartern loaf has
cost as much as 8*d*.

This question of
the price of the
quartern loaf is a
very important de-
tail, because of its
bearing on the la-
bourers' wages. Of
course both farmer
and labourer had to
bake their own
bread and provide
the firing, but the
baking was done by
lighting a fire of fag-
gots in the brick
ovens. After the
oven had been
heated in this way
the glowing ashes
were raked to the
sides, and then the
bread and pies were
put in, the iron door
closed, and the cook-
ing done by the im-
prisoned heat. The

Fig. 31.—Shoeing.

faggots or gorse were easily come by in the country.

So we can pass to the vexed question of the labourer's
wages. On our 300-acre farm two carters, a lad of seventeen and one boy were kept, who did the carting and
ploughing, and a shepherd (Fig. 26). There were three
labourers in addition, a groom-gardener and occasional
casual labour. Including the farmer's two sons, who
worked, this meant eleven people working on the

FIG. 32.—Sharpening the Scythe.

farm, in addition to the dairyman and his family, say fifteen in all on 300 acres, or one to every 20 acres. A good staff, but then eight cart-horses and two hunters were kept, and one old odd cart-horse and hack-driving horse and pony.

The labourers received 9s. to 10s. a week, and the carters and shepherd 1s. or so more. Extra on this each man received £2 for the harvest, and 10s. for haymaking, and there was a good supper and merry-making after hay-making or the harvest. Tipping was still very general, and they reckoned to pick up a good deal that way. Families were large, but the children soon began to earn wages and helped. Out of this the labourers paid 1s. a week for their cottages. Each cottage had its own garden, and the men were allowed extra ground on the farm to grow potatoes. All of them kept pigs, and the pig is a bounteous animal. Rabbits were bred in hutches, and others were wired on the farm. Readers of " Puck of Pooks Hill " will remember that old Hobden liked cold pheasant for breakfast, and it is pretty eating.

48

The labourers grew all the green stuff they wanted. So far as bread was concerned they were allowed to glean (Fig. 33), and many a labourer's wife and children would glean the equivalent of a sack of flour, or ninety quartern loaves, say the bread supply for three months. Nearly all the year round there was a chance of piecework for the labourer.

One point to be remembered is that, though the labourers' wages seem scandalous to us looking back now, they were accepted as fair then ; wages were scandalously low all round.

Still people did go hungry. We remember talking to an old farmer

FIG. 33.—Gleaning.

in Buckinghamshire, whose father had been a labourer and whose boyhood went back to about this time. His mother thought she would eke out the flour for the bread-making by adding barley meal. When she went to the oven to see the result of her experiment she found that all the loaves had ran into one large cake over the floor of the oven. This was so much of a tragedy that she sat down and wept, and then her husband came in. He went into the garden and got his spade and washed it, and then cut

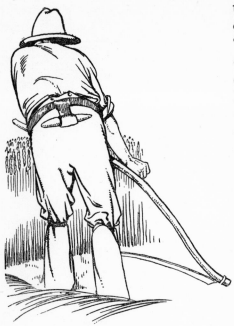

FIG. 34.—Reaping.

the cake of bread out of the oven. " Well," we asked the old farmer, " did you eat it ? " " Eat it ! " he replied. "I should think we did. Why, we were so hungry in those days we very nearly ate one another."

There was no great variation in the work on the farm, as detailed in Vol. III. Ploughing was done with an iron plough, and corn was sown with a drill and still cut with a scythe.

It is interesting to note that Hardy mentions the horse-drill as being a novelty at Casterbridge (Dorchester) as late as about 1846. Reapers had not come into very general use, and three men with scythes (Fig. 34) could cut 10 acres in a long summer's day working from sunrise to sunset. Mechanical threshers were used, but winnowing was still a separate operation. Labour was plentiful and cheap, and it had not yet occurred to the farmer that it was desirable to save labour.

This is a point to be noted—the number of people living on the land in 1872, and the variety of trades which could still be found in the English village. Our 300-acre farm, with three others, was grouped around a village of 600 inhabitants, which included the following occupations. There was the landlord, parson, and schoolmaster. Then the four farmers with their carters, shepherds and labourers. The farmers sent their corn to the water-mill to be ground into flour by the miller, and two bakers made bread and cakes for such as did not do their own baking. A butcher killed the local bullocks, and there was a pig-killer and pork butcher. The wheel-wright made the waggons (Figs. 38 and 39), and two blacksmiths shod the horses (Fig. 31) and re-paired the machinery, and one of them was the veterinary surgeon. A thatcher (Fig. 29) thatched the stacks, and a hurdlemaker (Fig. 28) made the hurdles for the sheep. A basket-maker made baskets for all pur-

FIG. 35.—Country-made Chair.

poses, and cradles for the babies out of the local willows. A carrier fetched and carried from the station and market town. A mason and bricklayer did the walling for houses, and two carpenters did the carpentering work and made the coffins, and they cut out their timber over a saw-pit (Fig. 37). They frequently made chairs (Fig. 35) and furniture as well. There were inns for refreshment, and of course the general shop for groceries. A tailor made the men's clothes and knew how to cut a good pair of breeches. The shoemaker did actually make good boots that would keep out the wet, and the dressmaker clothed the women. There were the gamekeepers, whom nobody liked, and the bird stuffer to deal with the rare bird, which of course was shot on first sight. The village, in fact, was like the farm and carried a good head of live stock.

It may pay us to look at the work of these village

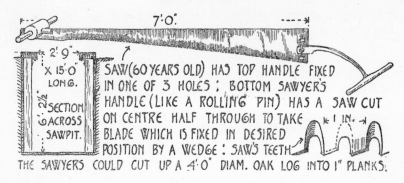

7'·0".

2'·9"
X 15·0"
LONG.

2½ SECTION
ACROSS
SAWPIT.

SAW(60 YEARS OLD) HAS TOP HANDLE FIXED
IN ONE OF 3 HOLES : BOTTOM SAWYER'S
HANDLE (LIKE A ROLLING PIN) HAS A SAW CUT
ON CENTRE HALF THROUGH TO TAKE
BLADE WHICH IS FIXED IN DESIRED
POSITION BY A WEDGE : SAWS TEETH

1 IN.

THE SAWYERS COULD CUT UP A 4'·0" DIAM. OAK LOG INTO 1" PLANKS.

Fig. 36.—The Pit Sawyer's Apparatus.

tradesmen in detail. Take the wheelwright who made the
waggons. We illustrated some in Vols. II and III, and
in the latter volume quoted from a letter we received from
Thomas Hardy in 1921, in which he referred to the Wessex
waggon as having a very marked curve, and being decorated
with floral designs on the front and tail-board which were
very ingenious. Ever since 1921 we were on the look-out
for a waggon decorated in this way, but with no success.
Then it occurred to us to write to the *Western Gazette* and
ask their assistance. They very kindly published our
letter, with the result that we discovered the waggons as
Figs. 38 and 39. It will be noted that the decorations are
as described by Thomas Hardy.

Fig. 30 shows the tools the thatcher uses, and Fig. 37
a saw-pit. Here again we have been fortunate. This was
still in use in 1934 and there cannot be many others.

All these people working together did produce a state
of society which was very complete and whole.

This brings us to something of which we shall have
more to say in our section on town-planning—how did
these simple folk and their forbears achieve anything so
fine as the old English village. Cobbett tells us how their
sites were selected. When he was going on his Rural
Rides from 1821 onwards, to find out how country life
was going then, he used to start at the source of a river

and then work down the valley. Good soil and water are required for the life of man and beast, and Cobbett, a farmer's son, knew that these are found by the side of the river more often than on the bare hill tops. Man fed his flocks on the Downs in Neolithic times, and watered them from ponds which stole their moisture from the dew, but when he discovered the use of iron and could make good tools he came downhill and cleared away the trees for his crops. An English village may well have 2000 years of history behind it. Its houses may have begun as the wattled and daubed huts of Glastonbury, and finished with the bungalow of to-day. But, leaving out this later horror, let us examine the village as it used to be a few years ago. The

FIG. 37.—Pit Sawyers at work at Rossway, Herts, in 1934.

53

FRONT WHEELS 3'-7" DIAM. BACK WHEELS 4'-9"~TRACK OVERALL 6'-4'~ BODY BLUE~
WHEELS & UNDERFRAMING RED~MADE BY KAIL OF HORTON DORSET IN 1873 VLS

Fig. 38.—Waggon belonging to Mr. S. R. Lush, Clapton Farm, Cucklington, Wincanton, Somerset.

FRONT WHEELS 3'-9" DIAM. BACK WHEELS 4'-6"~ TRACK OVERALL 5'-10"~ WHEELS & UNDERFRAMING RED~ BODY BLUE: MADE BY RICHARDS, STOBOROUGH, DORSET.

FIG. 39.—Waggon belonging to Mr. G. P. Foot, Hill Farm, Lytchett Minster, Dorset.

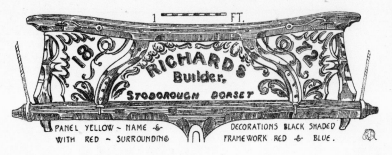

FIG. 40.—Tailboard of Mr. Foot's Waggon.

first thing which strikes us is the simplicity of the houses. A cottage is generally like a Noah's Ark—an oblong roofed in the simplest way. Take it out of its setting and transplant it elsewhere and its charm has gone. Attempt to imitate it in a suburb, and the result is terrible. The houses were helped by being built of local materials in tune with the countryside—but all this does not explain their charm. Centred in the village is the church, to minister to its spiritual life. Here again are centuries of tradition. St. Alban was martyred in England in A.D. 304, and many churches were built after the Edict of Toleration in 313. St. Martin's at Canterbury was a very old church already when Bertha welcomed Augustine there in 597. At Brixworth, in Northamptonshire, is a church in which people have worshipped Sunday by Sunday for 1300 years. The village blacksmith, who went to church and sat among his sons, and heard his daughter's voice singing in the village choir, did not go by himself. He was accompanied by the squire, farmers and all his friends. When they listened to the service in the church and the incomparable prose of the Bible, of how the sower went forth to sow, and the shepherd tended his flocks at night, every parallel illumined their own life and glorified it. Man does not live by bread alone—his spirit needs attention. The " 'ists," " 'isms " and " 'ics " go very well with the gloom of towns, but shrivel in the sunlight of the country. Miracles can be understood there, because the miracles of life and growth

56

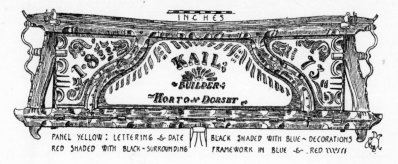

FIG. 41.—Tailboard of Mr. Lush's Waggon.

are always before the countryman's eyes. So when next you go to an English village, don't for heaven's sake call it " picturesque " and pass on—there is more to it than this. Things, like people, reflect their uses, and the old English village at its best is probably the most beautiful Everyday Thing we have produced so far. Perhaps this was the case because the life lived there was so natural, that man was at peace and seemed able to control his own fate.

William Barnes, the Dorset poet, gave us memorable pictures of this life which has passed away. Here is a verse from " Praise o' Do'set " :

" We Do'set, though we mid be hwomely,
Be'nt asheäm'd to own our pleäce ;
An' we've zome women not uncomely ;
Nor asheäm'd to show their feäce ;
We've a meäd or two wo'th mowèn,
We've an ox or two wo'th showèn,
In the village,
At the tillage,
Come along an' you shall vind
That Do'set men don't sheäme their kind.
Friend and wife,
Fathers, mothers, sisters, brothers,
Happy, happy, be their life !
Vor Do'set dear,
Then gi'e woone cheer ;
D'ye hear ? woone cheer ! "

57

SOCIAL

Passing to education, the labourers' children went to the village school and were taught the three R's, but then they lived in the midst of such an interesting little world that they absorbed general knowledge every day. The farmers' sons went to Wimborne Grammar School, where they received a classical education.

There was plenty of fun in the English village. It is the greatest mistake to think that life was, or is, dull there. The town is the inhuman place where no one knows anybody else, and you can die in your bed and remain there mummified and neglected. In the village life has to be led among your fellows, who are vitally interested in you. You will be talked about and your every weakness discussed, but you will not be neglected. To-day, with women's institutes and dances and all the other activities, the village is gayer than the town.

In 1872 there was village cricket, fêtes and the feasts of the various benefit societies. Markets were attended by the farmers and their wives, and at regular intervals there were fairs at Woodbury Hill and Poundbury, near Dorchester. Then on a winter's day the ploughman could have an "easy" as the hounds went by, and perhaps pick up a shilling by opening a gate for the weaker members of the hunt. As he went home at night he would meet a man jogging back and find out all the details of the day's run.

The labourer might get a job as a beater on a shoot, or have a day's rabbiting with his master, or do some ratting on his own, and ratting is an amusing sport.

Then we must not forget the Yeomanry, officered by the landlords and manned by their tenants' sons.

Once a year they all went to Weymouth, and the officers stayed at the very best hotel, and the men at the next best, and they all did themselves in first-rate style, with some soldiering in between times. The officers had to be very well mounted indeed, because many of their men would turn up with horses worth £200, and a groom to look after them. The Yeomanry was really the Hunt in military guise.

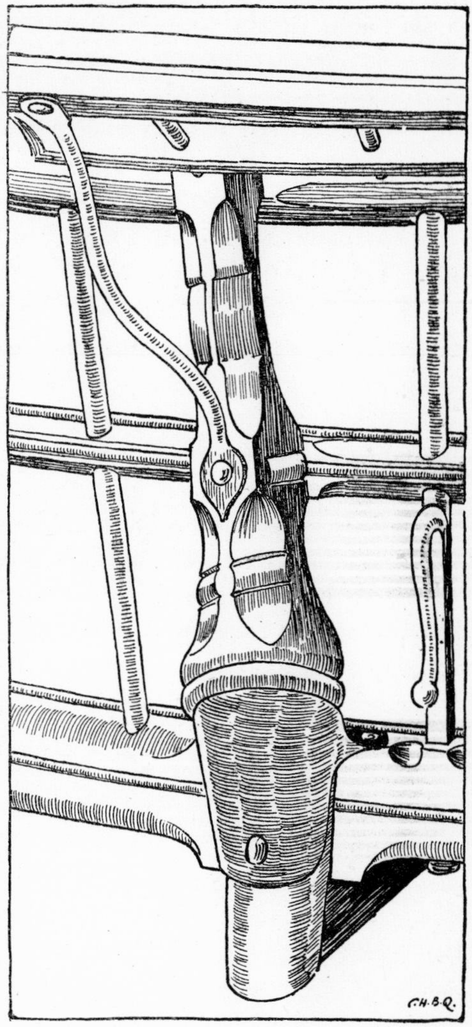

Then there was horse-racing, as perhaps the greatest passion, where men would see how they could get across country on a good horse.

It so happened that we spent a considerable portion of of our childhood on farms in Kent, and looking back we remember the old country people as great characters.

Here is a tale of a farmer's wife who, like her sovereign lady, Queen Victoria, disliked tobacco smoke. If her menfolk wanted to smoke it must be outside *her* house, be-

FIG. 42.—Strouter on Mr. Foot's Waggon.

cause the house *was* hers. Well, one day her husband came home from market. He was a sober man, but he did like to smoke a good cigar with his friends. It was late when he returned and his wife had gone to bed, but not to sleep, because the moment he entered the bedroom she smelt the cigar smoke, and ordered him to put his clothes outside the door in the passage as he took them off. Fortified by his recent association with male friends, he refused to do so and, putting his clothes on a chair, got into bed. His wife at once got out and, gathering his clothes together, put them out of the window, as she said, to sweeten them, and returned to bed. The husband, as so many men have, now found himself committed to an unequal contest with his wife ; so he rose and, gathering the old lady's clothes together, he put hers out of the window to keep his company, and found it a troublesome task, because she wore a crinoline, and this had to be pressed together before it would go through the narrow mullioned window, and it was not done at the first attempt. Then he returned to bed—but his wife was not distressed. She pointed out how shabby her clothes had been, and how it was only her consideration for his pocket which had prevented her buying new ones, but now she would have to have a complete outfit, and simulated sleep with an entirely gratuitous snore. The husband, feeling that the situation was getting beyond his control, now rose yet once more and announced loudly that he was going down to retrieve his own garments. The moment the wife heard him going down the stairs she rose up and ran to the window, and saw that the husband was very careful to gather up her clothes first, so that when he returned she did not accept his invitation to follow his example. Men are very much what their mothers and wives make them ; these women made fine men.

We can now move forward another generation and take the case of a young farmer of twenty-three, who took a water-mill in Dorset in 1879 and tried his hand at milling. The mill had two pairs of wheat and one pair of barley stones. 1879, when our miller began, was a disastrously wet season. The short revival of agricultural prosperity from 1867 to about 1874 was over.

In 1879 wheat had gone down to about 44s. the quarter. At two sacks to the quarter, one sack = 22s., and the

Fig. 43.—Throw the ball into the hole and "Up goes the Donkey."

(From sketch by Heywood Sumner.)

miller turned ten sacks of wheat, = £11, into seven sacks of flour for the same price, or about 31s. for a sack of flour. The ninety quartern loaves this produced cost then just over 4d. for the quartern, if the baking were done at home.

This was a very important consideration for the labourer's wife baking her own bread. As the result of the agitation of Joseph Arch, her husband's wages had been raised to 12s. a week, but the relief was to be of short duration, because in the 'eighties the foreign corn was to begin to pour into the country in an ever-widening and deepening stream. Landed at Bristol, it was ground

61

into flour in mills on the dockside, so that land in Dorset began to go out of cultivation. The labourers were given notice, and drifted to the towns ; the teams of horses were sold, and the smiths who had shod them found their occupation gone. Not all at once of course. Economic revolutions begin gradually, almost imperceptibly ; then in a few years life which was healthy and vigorous has declined.

Our young miller, who had started business in 1879, found that his milling now was not so profitable. He began to have to grind food for pigs instead of people, so in 1898 he bought a 200-acre farm, with farm-house, buildings and two cottages, for £3000, or £15 an acre, and put it all down to grass. Wheat was now only worth 12s. a sack, and you could buy cotton cake broken and bagged for £3 18s. a ton delivered, and the bags were free. So cows were kept instead of corn grown, and the price of cows went up. Cheese was not made, but the milk sent into the towns. The village shrank, and was only saved from extinction by growing watercress for the operatives in the manufacturing districts, who fancied this vegetable as an addition to their tea-table.

Here is another case, of a good arable farm of 800 acres which was to let in 1902. The only way in which the landlord could find a tenant was to grass it all down, and then put in a plant to pump the water up to a reservoir and lay on the water from this to each field. A cow drinks about ten gallons a day. After doing this the landlord was able to let the farm at £1 an acre, paying tithe, or half the rent of 1872.

This made things very difficult for the landlord as well as the farmer. Many of the old " resident native gentry," of whom Cobbett wrote as being " attached to the soil, known to every farmer and labourer from their childhood, frequently mixing with them in their pursuits where all artificial distinctions are lost, practising hospitality without ceremony from habit and not in calculation," had to pack up their traps and go. There was nothing new in this. The same thing had happened in Cobbett's time. The magnate (loathsome word) who had made money in industry, or by gambling on the Stock Exchange, sought to acquire gentility by buying land. Subconsciously he realized that he might civilize himself in this way, but the process was a painful one for all concerned. He did not realize, as Coke of Holkham did, that the land must be served with devotion, and thought of it instead as his playground.

The new landlord was a great sportsman, and mass-produced pheasants were slaughtered in thousands, and his sons and daughters rode to hounds. There are only three generations between clogs and clogs, or shirtsleeves and shirtsleeves, and this was the spending one. The wily old countryman, who would not have thought of trying it on the old landlord, did not hesitate to charge the new one top prices, and a bit over.

One of these new-fashioned gentry built himself a house in Surrey about the beginning of the century, and an amazing house it was. As the client did not know what he wanted, the house was altered and added to and turned inside out, until in the end it looked like an overgrown seaside hotel. The stables were better; there the problem of housing horses was tackled in a practical if gorgeous way. But the crowning folly was a smoking-room under a lake. It was thought that it would be amusing to watch the fishes while smoking Coronas, but the glass of course was quickly covered with scum, so that the room was only like a rather dank greenhouse. Hills were cleared away to obtain views, and money spent riotously; and then the smash came and the owner had to stand his trial for fraud, and committed suicide on being sentenced to a long term of imprisonment. The good land of England has suffered many indignities, and this was one. So things were until the war of 1914–18 brought a hectic prosperity to the countryside. Farmers made money once more and lost all sense of proportion; the tale is well told in " Farmer's Glory." Mr. A. G. Street has also given an excellent concise survey of farming shortly before the world war of 1939 in his *Farming England,* for which he went all over the land enquiring and noting conditions and methods, and a group of experts have shown the importance of agriculture and pointed out remedies for our defects and shortcomings in *England and the Farmer,* edited by H. J. Massingham and published in July, 1941.

In another farm of about 1200 acres the whole area is grassed down, and 120 dairy cows and 140 heifers graze the pastures and live out all the year round. The land is good and once grew corn. Now eleven men are employed, with casual labour for hay-making. Taking the regular labourers, the proportion is one man to every 109 acres—in 1872 on the 300-acre farm (p. 48) the proportion was one man to every 20 acres—which is one of the reasons that we have so many unemployed. An extraordinary method of living, my masters. The farm is no longer a farm, but a ranch. The face of England is being altered.

This practice of keeping cows out of doors all the year round was first begun by that farming genius A. J. Hosier, about 1920, and furthermore he invented an out-of-doors milking outfit. This consists of a movable shed, without any floor, in which the cows stand while they are being milked by a machine, which extracts the milk by suction. The cows soon get used to the outfit, because they discover that food is provided in it. The great benefits of the system are that the cows are healthier and do not suffer from tuberculosis ; expensive buildings are saved ; the cows do not have to be driven on to the high-roads to reach the milking place, and they deposit the manure themselves where it is needed—on the land. Poor land is improved. But the machine saves labour and does nothing to increase the number of people on the land, unless it is linked up with other occupations.

A. G. STREET

In A. G. Street's later book, "Land Everlasting," he suggests that this can be done by turning our attention from wheat to meat production, poultry, eggs, fruit and vegetable farming, in addition to dairy work. The Canadians grow better wheat than we can, so why waste money on the Quota ?—is Mr. Street's argument. Rather let us concentrate on the production of fresh food, which we can do better than anybody else. The main thing is to get more than one man on 20 acres, and so bring the villages back to life. But in war we must grow corn.

We know of one to-day which is forlorn, but originally it was as charming as the one described on p. 50. Soon after the first Great War the village was sold by the old landlord to a syndicate of speculators. This was a very frequent occurrence then—the town of Shaftesbury is another case. It was the inhabitants who were sold in reality, because the village was of no use to anyone without the inhabitants. However, they were allowed to purchase their cottages if they could raise the money, and the farm land went to a farmer, but certain fields were reserved for " development," with a resulting bungaloid growth in which old railway carriages figure.

The village became the haunt of literary men, artists and actors, and their pounds and a petrol pump helped to keep the cottagers going. The people fed on food brought to them from the most distant parts of the earth by the aid of the most scientific machinery. They can listen-in to the doings of all the peoples all over the earth—prime ministers will address them, and on Christmas Day they can travel all round the Empire and hear their King at the last—but the village as a village is dead.

FOOD FROM ABROAD

We had arrived then at this position, that good arable land in England was turned back into prairie like that in Canada, which was broken up to provide us with the corn we now import. We have traced how quietly and almost imperceptibly this has happened. It has been no man's fault, but the result of slow forces acting below the surface of life, and not easily seen.

The politicians of 1846 had little alternative but to repeal the Corn Laws. We have seen that this did not at once affect the English farmer, but by the 'eighties the import of corn reached such proportions that it did. By the courtesy of the High Commissioner for Canada we are enabled to publish Figs. 44 and 45, of a wheatfield in western Canada. Compare this with the 50 acres our Dorset farmer used to grow in 1872. Sixty odd years ago this Canadian wheatfield was prairie and the pasture ground for thousands of buffaloes. Even this wheatfield is out of date, because the corn has been cut with a reaper and binder. To-day machines have been invented which, owing to the dryness of the climate, make it possible to cut and thresh all in one operation and deliver the grain into a cart, as Fig. 45. The carts deliver it to the elevators as Fig. 46, and the elevators to the ships as Fig. 47. Now we can see what happens when the wheat arrives here.

FARMER AND FOOD (New Methods)

We have seen on p. 62 that it became a sounder policy, when foreign wheat began to be imported, not only to store it at the docks, but grind it into flour there as well. A great industry and wonderful machinery have been developed in doing this. Our example is the Millennium Flour Mills, at Victoria Dock, London (Fig. 51), which is the W. Vernon & Sons branch of Messrs. Spillers Ltd., and we are indebted for the information and illustrations to Messrs. Henry Simon Ltd., of Cheadle Heath, Stockport, who installed all the wheat-cleaning and flour-milling machinery there; this mill produces 100 sacks of flour of 280 lb. each for every hour of the twenty-four hours on six days of the week.

FIG. 44.—Wheatfield in Western Canada.

FIG. 45.—Cutting, threshing and delivering Wheat into Cart in
the Field.

[*By courtesy of the Canadian Government.*

FIG. 46.—Delivering the Wheat at an Elevator.

FIG. 47.—Loading the Wheat from the Elevator to Ship.

We will start with the unloading of the grain ship in the dock as plan, Fig. 48. The ship is discharged by a bucket elevator, which is plunged into the hold and takes as much wheat as will flow into it. Then the " Simon " travelling pneumatic plant, as Fig. 52, sucks the remainder of the grain out of the holds and delivers it into the conveyors shown in Fig. 52, in enclosed troughs in the quay. These go to the elevator house, and then across the bridge into the silos. This plant can handle 200 tons an hour, and the work can be done in any weather and the grain is kept dry. The silos hold 50,000 quarters of wheat, and this can be sorted out and placed in different bins. As it enters the silo it is weighed automatically by an Avery machine, 3000 lb. at a tip. As well the wheat receives a preliminary cleaning in transit on screening sieves. It can as well be received from the railway on the quay.

As some of the wheat is very dirty it needs to be cleansed. Other seeds may be mixed with it, together with straw, sticks, stones and old nails, which must be removed. So the first step in the manufacturing process is to take the wheat by conveyors to the cleaning department or screen room (see Fig. 48). Here it is weighed again on entry and passes into a separator, which consists of sieves and an air current which get rid of some of the impurities. The wheat then passes over electro-magnetic separators, which attract any nails or particles of iron or steel. Another dry-cleaning machine consists of a perforated cylinder with a central shaft on which are beaters that drive the wheat against the inside of the cylinder, which is serrated, and this scours the grain and removes adhering dirt and smut. Then there are separators that remove any foreign seeds like barley or oats. Sieves have already removed seeds which are narrower than wheat, but oats, which are of about the same width but are longer, still remain, so the Carter disc separator sorts the seeds into lengths. These foreign seeds are not thrown

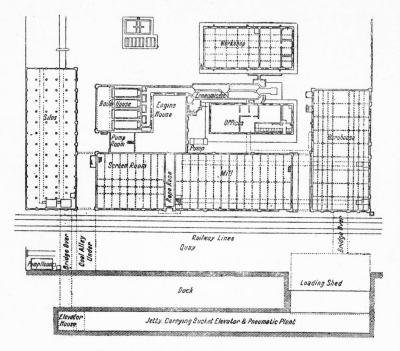

FIG. 48.—Plan of the Millennium Mills.

away, but sold; nothing is wasted in the mill. After passing through these dry-cleaning processes the wheat is taken by elevators to washing and stoning machines, which remove stones and dirt on the grain. Centrifugal whizzers remove the exterior moisture, and the wheat then passes to conditioning machines, which bring the wheat to the correct "condition" for milling into flour, and then brush machines, which give it a final polish and by air currents extract any particles of dust still remaining.

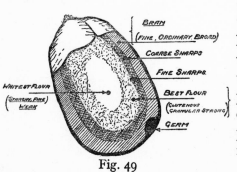

Fig. 49

The wheat is now

in a condition to pass into bins in the mill itself, as Fig. 48, but first we must remember that the public demands a white loaf. Fig. 49 shows how a grain of wheat is built up, and much of the ingenuity of the maker of modern milling machinery goes in removing anything like bran or sharps that would discolour the flour. This was not possible with the old stone mills. In the modern mill, instead of the wheat being ground between stones, the first process is to break it open be- tween steel rollers

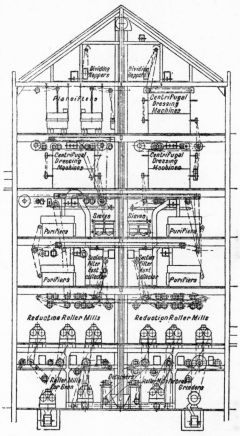

FIG. 50.—Section of the Millennium Mills.

which are grooved like a saw's tooth from end to end on a slight spiral. The rollers revolve, one rather faster than the other, and turn inwards. As the wheat falls between them it is cracked or broken open and a proportion of the floury contents released, and so the processes are continued until the wheat has resolved itself into round about 75 per cent. flour and 25 per cent. bran and offals. The flour is sacked, weighed and passed into the warehouse, where it can be stored or delivered into railway trucks, ships or barges, and throughout it has not been touched by human hands.

We can now turn to fruit. Only a few years ago boys and girls had to depend mainly on English fruit. The cherries, apples, pears and plums ripened in due season, and the imported oranges only appeared in time for Christmas, and were rather sour at first. To-day the fruits of the tropics are for sale, and the banana and grapefruit, which were once sold in Bond Street, are now seen on the costermongers' barrows, and mangoes come from India, and other fruit from South Africa.

There is a laboratory in Kent of biological engineering, with a model of a ship's hold, which contains 120 tons of fruit, which is tested as if in transit. Special ships are built for the trade so that the fruit may be kept fresh and succulent.

The same applies to meat, which now comes to us from all over the world. In 1846 we have seen that it was the possibility of famine which led to the repeal of the Corn Laws ; the same conditions made the English people look about for additional meat supplies. In 1860 and 1863 the Privy Council discussed starvation diseases, and in 1866 the Society of Arts appointed a committee to consider national food supply. Refrigeration was unknown then. Canned foodstuffs were prepared for explorers and sailing ships, and the old sailors called their tinned meat " Harriet Lane." The name came about in this way. There was once a watchman at a factory which canned meat who had a friend called Harriet Lane. She went to see him one night, and after drinking London gin together they had a quarrel, and in the course of it she got pushed into a vat of boiling meat. This was distinctly awkward for the watchman, so he stirred her up, and it was not till boot buttons and pins and other female belongings began to be found by sailors in the tins that suspicions were aroused and inquiries made. This was the old sailing ship men's account, and sometimes they called their tinned meat Slung Gullion, but what that meant we do not know.

There have been great developments in canning. In

Fig. 51.—View of the Millennium Mills, Victoria Docks, London.

[By courtesy of Messrs. Spillers Ltd. and Messrs. Henry Simon Ltd.

FIG. 52.—Pneumatic Unloading Plant.

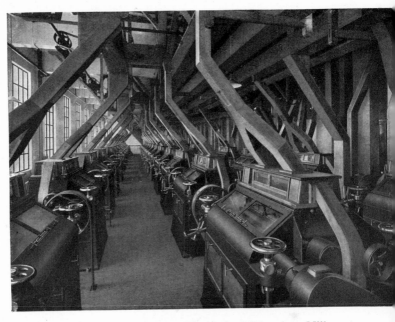

FIG. 53.—Roller Mills at the Millennium Mills.

[By courtesy of Messrs. Spillers Ltd. and Messrs. Henry Simon, Lt

1870 only 6000 people were so employed in the U.S.A., and in 1929 100,000. Australian tinned mutton was shown at the Great Exhibition, 1851, and was beginning to be known to the British public by the year 1867, and now we have made a very wide range in canning for ourselves.

Then about 1874 live cattle began to be brought over on the cattle boats, and readers of " Captains Courageous " will remember the delightful encounter which the *We're Here* had with one in mid-Atlantic, and how Uncle Salters, who was half farmer and half sailor, outraged Disko Troop by asking the skipper of the cattle boat what he fed his charges on while at sea. Disko asked Salters, " Can't ye never keep things sep'rate ? " Our sympathies have always been with Salters, because it is just the kind of fool question we should have asked ourselves.

But canning meat and bringing over live cattle on boats did not solve the problem of how to increase the food supply at home, and here the politicians were confronted with a tremendously difficult problem. They could have increased the home supplies by settling more men on the land, but this could only be done at the expense of the town industries. If you wish to build up a large export trade you must be prepared to accept in exchange for your manufactured goods raw materials or foodstuffs. Naturally you would not import other manufactured goods to compete with your own. In the 'seventies England was too deeply committed to Industrialism to contemplate any form of land settlement in England, because this would have drawn men from the factories and reduced the supply of labour necessary to produce the goods we wished to export. It was inconceivable to the manufacturers of that period that there might come a time when the foreign countries would prefer to manufacture their own goods, and the system of exchange might break down. So all the endeavour went in the direction of importing food.

Refrigeration by means of pumping the heat out of an insulated chamber had been discovered about 1850, but its practical application to food supplies had to wait for many years.

This was the work of two men, James Harrison, who was born in Glasgow in 1816, and emigrated to Sydney, Australia, in 1837, and Thomas Sutcliffe Mort, born 1816, at Bolton in Lancashire, who also went to Australia in 1838.

Harrison and Mort, who knew of the scarcity at home, were confronted with the waste in good meat which went on in Australia. Here the golden fleece of the sheep was more valuable than the carcass. The wool was exported to England, and the meat was boiled for tallow and then thrown away.

Mort built the first freezing works in the world at Sydney in 1861, and spent a large fortune in pioneer work. Harrison invented freezing machines, and exhibited frozen carcasses at Melbourne in 1873. Both men failed in the test of the sea voyage back to England. Their work, however, led to the first cargo of beef, which came over from Australia in 1880 by the steamship *Strathleven*, of 2436 tons, as Fig. 54. Some mutton was included in the cargo, and it arrived in London in good condition in February, 1880. A carcass of lamb was sent to Queen Victoria, and a sheep to the Prince of Wales, who declared that the meat was good.

By 1882 the trade had spread to New Zealand, and in that year mutton was sent to us in the sailing clipper *Dunedin*, as Fig. 55. The voyage took ninety-eight days. The carcasses were stowed in chambers made in the hold and roughly insulated by melted tallow run between bulkheads. A steam engine drove the heat pump, which was an ammonia compressor. The voyage was successful.

The Argentine then hastened to share in the meat trade with England, and they started sending frozen carcasses in 1883, and by 1901 their chilled meat industry had become firmly established. This means that the meat was not frozen as hard as a board, but just chilled. As chilled meat is superior to the frozen, the Argentine began to cut

Fig. 54.—The *Strathleven*, the Steamship that brought the first Cargo of Frozen Meat to England from Australia.
(From a painting in the possession of Messrs. Burrell & Son, Glasgow.)

Fig. 55.—The *Dunedin*, the Sailing Vessel that brought the first cargo of Frozen Meat to England from New Zealand.

[*By courtesy of Messrs. Shaw Savill and Albion Co., Ltd.*

into the Australian trade, so the scientists got to work to see if they could discover how chilled meat could be brought from Australia.

The operative in the industrial town, who buys his Sunday joint on Saturday night so cheaply, does not realize the amount of scientific research which has been carried out to make the purchase possible. The Report of the Food Investigation Board for the year 1932 details the laboratory experiments carried out by the Low-Temperature Research Station at Cambridge which made possible the recent shipment of chilled beef from New Zealand.

Apparently the storage life of chilled beef in plain air is limited by the growth of micro-organisms which produce a taint in the fat. It was then discovered by experiment that this growth of the moulds and bacteria, commonly found on chilled beef, could be retarded and the storage life doubled if it were kept in an atmosphere charged with small quantities of carbon-dioxide. The beef as well looked better and retained its bloom, and the gas had no harmful effect on the flavour of the meat. This being the case, the shippers at once got to work, and an experimental shipment was made from New Zealand to this country. The animals were slaughtered with the greatest care and all possible precautions taken against bacterial contamination. This was a very important detail, because meat from a dirty old slaughter-house suffers far more chance of contamination than that from a modern abattoir. Five hundred and twenty hindquarters were selected and put into coolers for chilling for five or six days, and then taken out and loaded into the *Port Fairy* as quickly as possible. The gas chamber was an experimental one between decks, cooled by brine grids, and fitted with a fan to circulate the air, charged with 10 per cent. of carbon dioxide.

The *Port Fairy* left Wellington on June 9th, 1933, and encountered bad weather, which led to some escape of gas, but, notwithstanding this, the meat was discharged at

Southampton on July 18th in good condition, free from mould and bacterial growth. It was sold in Smithfield Market forty-nine days after it had been slaughtered in New Zealand, and realized 3s. to 3s. 4d. per stone. Details of the *Port Fairy* shipment are given in *Ice and Cold Storage* for August, 1933.

One important result in this carriage of meat in carbon dioxide is that it will enable it to be sent right across the world and through the tropics by countries like Australia and New Zealand in a chilled state, whereas before it had to be frozen hard. In this way the Empire can compete with the Argentine.

We think that the reports of the Food Investigation Board might well be added to secondary school libraries. They would help to give the work done in the laboratories more sense of reality. A boy or girl may well say, " What is the importance of this work I am given to do ? " The reports answer the question. Here are some of the subjects which are dealt with : The Effect of Ethylene on the Respiration and Sugar Content of Potatoes ; The Bio-chemical Study of Senescence in Apples ; Chemical Changes in the Fat of Bacon during Storage ; Effect of Temperature of Storage on the Denaturation of the Globulin of Haddock's Muscle frozen in Brine at — 20° C.

Let us consider some of the results to date of these experiments at Cambridge. Had we gone there a year or so ago and seen equal weights of minced frog's muscle being placed in tubes, we might have been just amused and not have realized at all the significance of the test. Here is the first result. *The Times* of January 6th, 1934, gave an account of a party which was held on board the *Port Chalmers* in King George V Dock, in London, to give a good send-off to that ship on her first voyage. This twin-screw motor-vessel, built for the Commonwealth and Dominion Line, was the first of nine for the New Zealand food trade, and she had her holds fitted with special gas-tight chambers for the carriage of chilled beef. This means work for many others beside the shipbuilders—miners, engineers, electricians and many others will be called in to assist and trade generally will be improved.

Here are some figures which show how vast the food trade is. New Zealand alone in 1923 exported to this country 1,250,140 cwt. of butter, 1,441,460 cwt. of cheese, and 6,400,000 carcasses of lamb and mutton. In 1941 these figures had risen to 2,637,683, 2,033,506 and 13,189,200 respectively, and pork and bacon is being added. The frog who laid down his life and gave his muscle to Cambridge little knew the high destiny before him when he wriggled as a little tadpole in some pond.

The chemist has helped in other ways. He not only pays great attention to artificial fertilizers and the production of chemicals to destroy insect pests, but makes foodstuffs as well. Various oils, like those derived from linseed, soya beans and coco-nuts, though unpalatable by themselves, are nourishing when resolved into solid fats as margarine. What is not so pleasant is that the chemist can obtain various flavouring essences from coaltar which resemble the tastes of fruits. With these and some pulped turnip and artificial pips the unscrupulous manufacturer made jam—until the law stepped in. Sugar, again, is now extracted from the sugar beet as well as the sugar cane. One comforting reflection is that food factories are much cleaner places now than they used to be.

Then there have been enormous extensions in the catering trade. At the beginning of our period there were chop houses and a few restaurants for well-to-do people, but the poor only had the public-house, which was beastly. The first step seems to have been taken by the Aerated Bread Co., who started as bakers in 1862. In the early 'eighties the manageress of one of the bread shops obtained permission to serve cups of tea to customers. The experiment was a great success, and the result was the development of the A.B.C. tea-shops. Joseph Lyons was another benefactor ; he opened his first tea-shop at 213 Piccadilly on September 20th, 1894. Out of these shops have developed the Palace Hotels and palatial Corner Houses, where people of the most moderate means can live and feed in surroundings of splendour. Shops have followed suit and now have restaurants, and in peace well-to-do people entertain in hotels instead of their own homes. We are beginning to live more in common.

The second world war has brought home to us once again more acutely than before how vital to existence are the sea communications of our little island, with its huge population largely dependent on overseas food supplies, and how open these are to ruthless submarine and air-bombing attack. We have to do without many kinds of imported food which are pleasant but not indispensable, and live more simply and sparingly like our great-grand-parents, and as graphically described in *Piers Plowman*, it is necessary to wait till the harvest ripens for much of our fruit supply such as apples, for which in peace times we were largely independent of seasons. The Ministry of Agriculture induced the farmers to plough up an additional 1,542,236 acres in the season of 1939-40, with further large increases in the two following, so that the acres under cultivation have risen from 8,935,000 in 1939 to over 16,000,000 in October, 1941. This, with the countless allotments and gardens, means that Britain is producing from the soil far more than ever in her history. What can and will be arranged in the future is a problem for time to solve, but it is unlikely that farming will suffer the sad neglect of the post last war years, and we may perhaps hope that vision and foresight will be brought to bear on the crucial question of producing a large proportion of the nation's food at home.

Dr. Johnson was right when he said : " There is no way of living without the need of foreign assistance but by the product of our own land (or Empire), improved by our own labour. Every other source of plenty is perishable and casual."

CHAPTER III

THE BUILDER AND BUILDINGS

W HEN we come to the second of the three great primary trades the first question which arises is, whether we shall treat of the buildings or the towns first. The answer surely is the towns.

This was the great nineteenth-century mistake. They looked on towns as accumulations of buildings, and, as we have seen, we had to wait until the twentieth century, when Ebenezer Howard with his garden city, and John Burns with his 1909 Act, emphasized the necessity for town-planning. The nineteenth-century method when more houses were wanted was to buy a field, run some roads through it and build the houses. If these latter complied with the local by-laws as regards thickness of walls, heights of rooms and the provision of the necessary

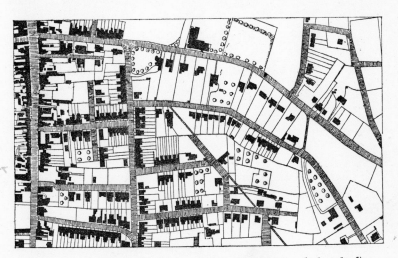

FIG. 56.—Nineteenth-century Town-planning (roads hatched).

sanitary accommodation, all was well; but the roads themselves need not be planned or connected up with other roads, or be part of a system. The amenities were not considered. Fig. 56 shows the suburban development of an English provincial town in the nineteenth century. It was all done in bits, without any plan, and looks like the handiwork of monkeys, not men.

This question of the design of towns is a very interesting one, because there is more to it than just design or planning. The town will reflect the uses to which it is put, and the character of the builders; towns, like houses, have their own aura. When you go into the matter you will find that just as in Europe there are only two kinds of civilization, Greek and Gothic, so there are only two kinds of towns, following these. Take the Glastonbury Lake Village, which came to an end just before the Roman occupation of Britain, and which we illustrated in our book on the " New Stone, Bronze and Early Iron " period. This was followed by Silchester, which we illustrated in " Everyday Life in Roman Britain." Glastonbury was the work of people without any idea of planning—it had grown just anyhow. Silchester shows how the Romans had absorbed Greek ideas and learned to plan well-ordered cities.

The forum in the centre, with its basilica, speaks of stable government. Then the Dark Ages came in, and when the town appears again it is strongly walled, with a frowning castle as its dominant feature, and the streets inside are narrow lanes that wriggle about without any plan. The barbarian Anglo-Saxons cared very little for planning. This was the Gothic civilization. We have never originated anything which could not be traced back to Greek or Gothic, nor have we made very much advance.

Take the City of London after the Fire of London in 1666. Wren prepared a plan for its rebuilding, and had the citizens adopted this we should have a noble city now— but it was not to be. The seventeenth-century Londoners were in a hurry; plans were a nuisance. They wanted to rebuild as soon as possible, so that they could stick up notices outside that " Business as Usual " was being carried on. They argued that, if they listened to this visionary Wren, they might actually lose money, and this was not to be thought of.

Moving to more recent times, Fig. 58 shows cotton mills with the work-people's dwellings grouped around them. Fig. 59 is of Tooting, a suburb of London, and explains what the modern garden city tries to avoid. Fig. 61 is of the old-fashioned, comfortable suburb for well-to-do people, and Fig. 60 of a modern housing scheme. Here are different kinds of town-planning.

Now as to the point of these remarks. Civilization comes from the Latin word for city, so to be civilized means to have learned how to live in a city at peace and in amity with your fellow-citizens in urbane fashion. Cities then are of prime importance in that they will show how far the citizens have progressed along this path. So far as England is concerned, and judged by our industrial cities, a very short distance indeed.

We have dealt already with the English village, and there can be little doubt that this is the best of the everyday things we have produced. The market town, where it was the metropolis or mother city of the countryside, could be very good where it fulfilled Hardy's definition : " Casterbridge was the complement of the rural life around, not its urban opposite."

That is about as far as we have got in the direction of being civilized. The village and its market town were successes because they were both real things, serving a useful purpose, and built on the solid foundation of agriculture.

When we come to the larger towns and cities we must examine their uses. London, which Cobbett so aptly described as the Wen, was possible in the eighteenth century. The city in those days was the market town for the country, and Westminster the seat of government.

Hampstead, Highgate and Streatham were villages, and in between were fields where the citizens could refresh and recreate themselves. Now all the fields have gone and these areas are filled up with dismal nineteenth-century buildings, shabby and forlorn. Do not judge London by its centre, or the outer ring of its most recent development, but spend a day in a circular trip on a radius of about three miles. The clerks who work in the City now live perhaps ten or twelve miles from their work, so that life in the inner ring is dwindling; it is the area of grubby lodging-houses and slums in the making, and what is to happen here no man knows. Occasionally a chunk of it will make a desperate effort at some kind of unity and announce that it has formed itself into a borough. A royal duke will come down and present a charter, and the traffic is held up for his coming, and at his going it rolls on and the borough remains as a blot.

This dismal area might be turned into a central park, as Ebenezer Howard's plan (Fig. 57), and all the railways stopped outside it and connected to Tubes underground. This has been done in New York with the Central Station. If all the London termini and hideous viaducts in the centre of London were pulled down the site values could go against the cost of the central park.

When we turn to the purely manufacturing towns which arose in the nineteenth century, these have been just frankly hideous from start to finish. Their only foundation is trade. The citizens may be engaged in the production of hairpins, and the women determine to wear their hair short, so the reason for the existence of the town has gone. It dwindles and disappears like Tyre, Sidon and Carthage. No stable civilization can be built solely on trade and industry.

To give the industrialists their due, two schemes must be mentioned that made valiant attempts to improve matters. Bournville was founded in 1879, and Port Sunlight in 1888. Here the old English village was clearly the inspiration, but neither had any life of their own and were only dormitories attached to factories.

One of the first people to realize that all was not well with Industrialism was the American writer, Edward Bellamy, who wrote " Looking Backward," in 1887. Bellamy must have been voicing the feelings of many, because his book achieved a great popularity and sold a million copies. Our interest in it is that, as we shall see on p. 83, it influenced our Ebenezer Howard, and can be taken as one of the things which caused a garden city to be built at Letchworth, in England.

The hero of Bellamy's tale, Julian West, suffers from insomnia and, going to sleep in Boston, U.S.A., in 1887, sleeps for 113 years, 3 months and 11 days, and so awakens in the year 2000. The book tells of all the things he finds then. He goes on to the roof top, and Boston is beneath him : " At my feet lay a great city. Miles of broad streets, shaded by trees and lined with fine buildings, for the most part not in continuous blocks, but set in larger or smaller enclosures, stretched in every direction. Every quarter contained large open squares filled with trees, among which statues glistened and fountains flashed in the late afternoon sun. Public buildings of a colossal size and an architectural grandeur unparalleled in my day raised their stately piles on every side." There is no smoke, because all heating and cooking is done by electricity. The city has become so prosperous that it has surplus wealth to spend in its adornment for the pleasure of all.

The kindly Dr. Leete, who looks after West, tells him how this has all come about. In the nineteenth century the use of machinery added enormously to production, and the small handicraftsman was crushed out of existence and found himself working for the employer who had the necessary capital. Then the concerns got larger still and the individual employer was swallowed up by a syndicate. Then as more capital was wanted people bought shares, and as the swallowing process was continued the number of concerns kept on getting smaller, and the number of shareholders larger, until at the final swallow there was only one left, the State, with all the citizens as shareholders.

West is sceptical in true nineteenth-century manner, but Leete reminds him that when the conditions of human life change the motives of human action change with them. War has disappeared in A.D. 2000, and the principle of universal military service has been adopted to fight the real enemies of hunger, cold and starvation.

All the people have the very best education that is possible, and it is based, not on the production of snobs, but on the principle of discovering if there are any tanners' sons, like Pasteur, who can serve the State. Education is continued till twenty-one, and great care is taken to discover true vocations. At twenty-one all pass into the industrial army and work as labourers for three years. All the rough work is done in this way, and it sweats the grease out of the young men and prevents them from being a nuisance. These are the privates, who after this three years can rise from the ranks—but all get the same pay. At forty-five they retire. All the products of labour pass into the national storehouses. There is no money, or buying, or selling. The merchants and the bankers and the middlemen go.

Each individual is given a credit card for his work, which he spends as he will at the national storehouses, and, freed from the fear of poverty, men have expanded and their intellects blossomed. As well there is no longer any necessity for the citizen to clutter himself up with many possessions. In the old days these were a safeguard against poverty, now they are merely an embarrassment. Each citizen has his house, and there are no servants ; but the family has its own room in the great dining hall and pleasure house attached to its quarter. Home life is simple, but social life luxurious. All washing is done in public laundries. The world has become a paradise for women in A.D. 2000.

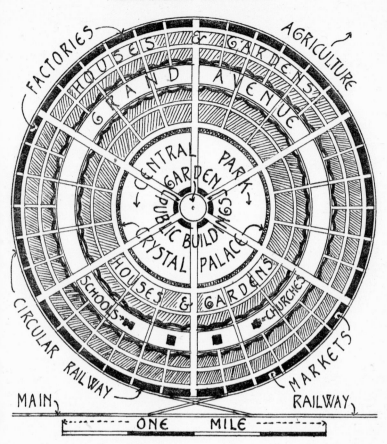

Fig. 57.—Howard's Plan for a Garden City, from "To-morrow."

Bellamy works out all the details in the most ingenious way. It was a great intellectual feat to have looked so far ahead in "Looking Backward," and it seems to-day as if many of the things Bellamy foretold will have happened by A.D. 2000. The interest to us, however, is that Bellamy seems to have been one of the causes of inspiration to the confectioner's son, Ebenezer Howard, with whom we now propose to deal.

Howard was born in London and, leaving school when he was fifteen, went into various City offices as a clerk. He then tried his luck in America, but, returning, later

83

became a reporter in the House of Commons. He had no influential friends behind him.

The importance of Howard's work is that it cannot be dismissed as Utopian. When "To-morrow" was published, in 1898, *The Times*, in its review, said, "The only difficulty is to create such a city, but that is a small matter to Utopians." It was no small matter, but as a result of the book Letchworth Garden City came to be built. Some men bend all their energies to making money —others paint pictures—a few misguided individuals write books, but how few leave a city behind them as a memorial. This is what Howard did, and he is the father of English town-planning. He looked on the industrial city, with its back-to-back slum houses and air of general confusion, and saw that it was vile and only fit to be abandoned.

Howard did not favour the creation of garden suburbs planted in the outer ring of existing towns. He realized that this is a very expensive form of development, with its miles of roads and sewers, that it means long journeys for the inhabitants to get to their work, and that it is impossible to make such a place into any centre of social life. Howard's ideal was : " A Garden City is a town designed for healthy living and industry, of a size which makes possible a full measure of social life, but not larger : surrounded by a rural belt : the whole of the land being in public ownership or held in trust for the community."

So in the scheme outlined in his book Howard suggested that 6000 acres of land should be bought in the country at what was a fair price in 1898 for agricultural land, £40 the acre, or £240,000, and the estate was to be placed in the hands of trustees and held by them for the benefit of the community. All the details of how the money was to be raised on mortgage, and the costs of so doing, and laying out the roads, and so on, are worked out in the most careful detail, and should be studied in " To-morrow." Of the 6000 acres, 1000 are devoted to the city itself, and the other 5000 remain as farms to supply the

FIG. 58.—Workpeople's dreary Dwellings huddled round the
Mills in a Lancashire Cotton Town.

FIG. 59.—The monotonous Terraces of a late Victorian Dormitory
Suburb : Tooting, London.

FIG. 60.—A Workmen's Housing Estate in Yorkshire laid out on a Circular Plan.

FIG. 61.—An Air View of the spacious Comfort of a well-to-do Victorian Suburb in South-west London.   Cf. Fig. 59.

[*Both by courtesy of Aerofilms Ltd.*

foodstuffs. Industry was not to be divorced from agriculture, but married to it.

Howard's plan for the garden city itself, as Fig. 57, is very novel, and extraordinarily interesting when you remember that he was a layman. The main line of the railway branches off to a station, and from this a circular railway runs round the city, and adjoining it are all the factories, coal and timber yards, and so on. There are no hideous railway viaducts inside the city, as there are in South London for one example. The city is bisected by six great boulevards, 120 feet wide, which run to the centre, where there is a garden, and around this are the public buildings, like the town hall, museum, theatre and library. These are seen across the greenery of the central park, and this is surrounded in the most amusing way by a crystal palace or large glazed walk. Here on wet days the citizens could walk, and there are shops to look at, and winter gardens with flowers.

The houses are on the avenues, and set in the midst of these is the Grand Avenue, 425 feet wide, and here are the schools and churches and playgrounds.

Now as to what was at the back of Howard's mind. We have seen that when he returned from America he became a reporter in the House of Commons. As such he would have listened to the interminable discussions there, and have known all the difficulties which attend attempts to remedy matters in old towns because of the vested interests. Take London, for example; within living memory land at Hampstead was worth only £600 to £700 an acre, and within a few years, because of the outward growth of London, the price was as many thousands. The same thing happened between Golders Green and Edgware when the Tube was extended. In London itself land is generally let on lease, and at the expiration of this the leaseholder has to pay a premium, a higher ground rent, and very likely rebuild the premises and pay higher rates on the improvements, which is comforting if you are the landlord, but trying if you wish to town plan or effect improvements. This increase of value to the landlord, caused solely by the increase of population, has been called his " unearned increment," and it is a fair term. Land has little value unless it carries a good head of human live stock which can be chained to it.

So Howard's idea was to escape all this by taking his workers into the country. He assumed that his 6000 acres had supported a population of 1000 before he bought it, and that these tenants paid £8000 a year rent, or £8 each. He argued that if he could build a garden city for 30,000 inhabitants, with 2000 on the surrounding land, the rent they would pay as ground rent, if divided up between them, would be negligible, and, if it could be so arranged that the community as a whole could benefit by the improvement, then such money could be spent on making the city a lovely place. This seemed quite possible, because each of the 32,000 inhabitants would only have to pay, say, £8 a year each, as the former 1000 did, to produce an annual income of £256,000, and this would be amply sufficient to pay the interest on the capital expenditure, and for the provision of a sinking fund.

The history of all the preliminary spadework is well told in Macfadyen's " Sir Ebenezer Howard and the Town-Planning Movement," and interesting sidelights are thrown on the character of this practical Utopian, and the first Mrs. Howard, as she was in those days before the knighthood, was a real helpmate. How this couple translated their dream into reality is the heroic part of the tale. " Now faith is the substance of things hoped for, the evidence of things not seen." Howard had faith ; he was transparently honest and entirely disinterested, and because of this was able to persuade people to help him, so that the foundation of the first garden city at Letchworth, in Herts, was carried out in 1903.

The estate which was bought at Letchworth had an area of 4562 acres, and this was bought at £40 15s. per

FIG. 62.—Children at Play in Howard Park, Letchworth.

FIG. 63.—A Corner by the Golf Course, Letchworth.

[*Both by courtesy of First Garden City, Ltd.*]

FIG. 64.—Interior of converted Warehouse used as a Dwelling-house, taken in a Northern Industrial Town in 1933.

FIG. 65.—Slum Courtyard in Northern Industrial Town (1933), since demolished. Note narrow Entrance Passage at bottom.

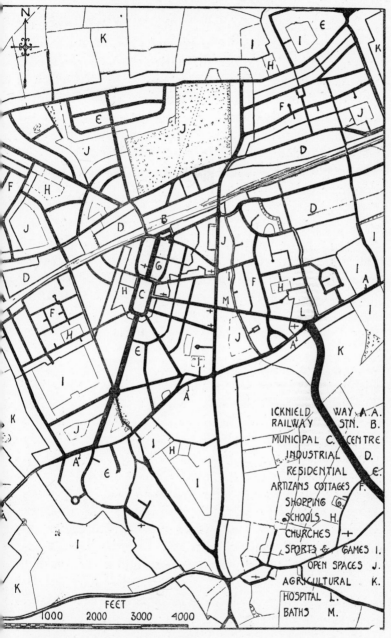

ICKNIELD WAY A.A.
RAILWAY STN. B.
MUNICIPAL C. CENTRE
INDUSTRIAL D.
RESIDENTIAL E.
ARTIZANS COTTAGES F.
SHOPPING G.
SCHOOLS H.
CHURCHES +
SPORTS & GAMES I.
OPEN SPACES J.
AGRICULTURAL K.
HOSPITAL L.
BATHS M.

FEET
1000   2000   3000   4000

FIG. 66.—Central Portion of First Garden City, Letchworth.
(*Barry Parker and Raymond Unwin, Architects.*)

G   87

acre. Plans were prepared by Messrs. R. Barry Parker and Raymond Unwin for a central town of 1500 acres, the remainder being left for agricultural purposes, and they have kindly lent us the plan of the city which is here reproduced as Fig. 66. The first point which may arise in the minds of our readers is that Howard did not carry out his plan as Fig. 57 at Letchworth; but ideal plans are seldom possible in practice. The estate which was bought there was bisected by the railway and Icknield Way, the oldest road in England; both these had to be preserved, and this applied as well to Norton Common, on the north of the railway. The municipal centre was placed near the railway, as were the factories, and these are on the north-east of the town, so that the prevailing south-west wind blows the smoke away. Great care was taken with the workmen's cottages. These are arranged not too far away from the workshops, but there are never more than twelve houses to the acre, and all have gardens. The work done in cottage building has influenced similar work done since all over England. The roads are lined with trees, and open spaces and playing fields are provided. The town has been town-planned.

The dividend payable to the shareholders is limited to 5 per cent., and after this is paid any increment in value comes back to the citizens, and nothing short of an Act of Parliament can prevent this. The city was only founded in 1903; all the roads have had to be made; the water, gas and electricity undertakings all belong to First Garden City Ltd. As time goes on and these capital charges are liquidated, and the city continues to grow, the increase in value may become very important and a great asset to the citizens.

As to the progress which has been made: the population in 1911 was 5324; in 1921, 10,313; in 1928, 14,080; in 1939, (estimated) 18,223. There are 3897 inhabited houses, 161 shops, 50 factories, 65 workshops, 17 churches, 5 hotels, and 6 places of amusement.

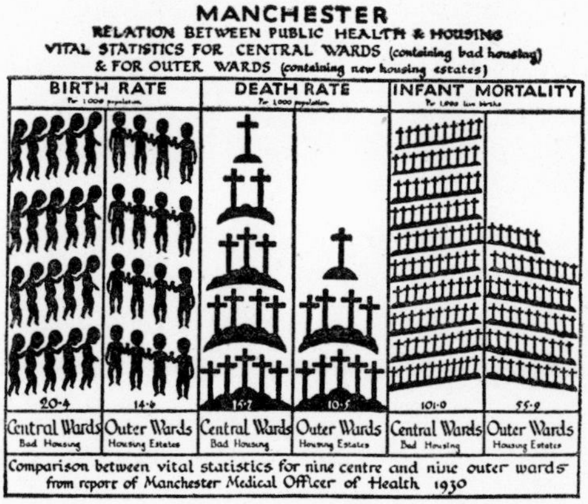

We publish Fig. 62, of the children's paddling pool in Howard Park, at Letchworth, because we think it catches the spirit of the place—children can be happy there—and Fig. 63 shows one of the pleasant corners.

FIG. 67.—Chart of Vital Characteristics.

Howard was a great man, and Letchworth one of the most vital things which has ever been produced in England.

Here is the very best kind of history. It is not concerned with war and destruction, but hope and construction.

SLUMS

Our readers, having arrived so far, may feel inclined to say, " What tiresome people these authors are ! Why will they keep harping on the subject of slums, especially as they have shown us that Ebenezer Howard solved the problem at the beginning of the century ? " Our answer to this is that, though Howard pointed the way, it was not followed. Slums still remain with us, and there is little real acknowledgment of the importance of town-planning. Look at Figs. 64 and 65. These photos were taken in 1933, and, happily, most of the inhabitants in this particular scheme have now been moved into nice new houses. Unhappily, many other slum areas remain. The Government was recently engaged in a five-years' clearance programme, which was concerned with 266,851 slum houses, occupied by approximately 1,240,182 persons. Fig. 67 shows the difference which good housing makes in the lives of people.

But the slum question is not only concerned with the clearance of slum areas. The slum is the scrap-heap of Industrialism. Unless the conditions of life and industry are improved, new slums will be created as fast as the old ones disappear.

Look at the children in Fig. 64. They are not any different to yourselves; they are fellow human beings. The Almighty did not create a lower order of beings who like to live in slums. They arrive there by a perfectly obvious process. A farm is laid down to grass; an industry dwindles; a new labour-saving machine is installed. Economically it may mean a few pounds in somebody's pocket, but more often than not it means a few more inhabitants in a slum area; and it may happen to any of us.

And the remedy? Well, the remedy is a very simple one—we have only to play the game of life as fairly as a game of cricket.

PUBLIC BUILDINGS

Having dealt with town-planning, we can now turn to the public buildings of the period, and we will begin with their design, and the battle of the styles. We saw in Vol. III that Pugin exhibited furniture of Gothic character at the Great Exhibition of 1851, and " Gothic " had been going strong since Walpole built his little Gothic castle at Strawberry Hill about 1750. Scott, Street and Butterfield were the leading Gothicists at the beginning of our period, and Scott's architecture was poor, lifeless stuff; the others had power and originality, but had set themselves a difficult and almost hopeless task.

Scott owed his conversion to Pugin's writing, and said, " I was a new man, old things had become new, or rather modernism had passed away from me, and every aspiration of my heart had become mediæval."

Again, we saw in Vol. III that Stuart and Revett published their book on the Antiquities of Athens, in 1762. This started a Greek fashion, which again lasted

FIG. 68.—Gothic Design submitted by George Gilbert Scott in the Competition for the Foreign Office Buildings, London, held in 1857.

(*R.I.B.A. Journal, Nov.,* 1933)

FIG. 69.—View from St. James's Park of the Foreign Office Buildings, London, as carried out by George Gilbert Scott.

[R.I.B.A. Journal, Nov., 1933

into our period. Elmes died in 1847, and Cockerell finished off his St. George's Hall at Liverpool. Tite was another classic man and designed the Royal Exchange, London.

So the architects were divided into two camps, and feelings ran high. The periodical election of the President of the Royal Institute of British Architects gave them an opportunity to demonstrate their principles. Sometimes their votes carried a Gothic man to the presidential chair, and at others a Classic man was successful. Sir William Tite, who was born in 1798, and died 1873, was twice President of the Royal Institute of British Architects, and a leading Classicist. In his will he left £1000 to found a prize to be awarded annually for the study of Italian architecture.

Then an amusing thing happened. A competition was held in 1857 for the new Foreign Office, in Whitehall, London, and this was won by George Gilbert Scott, with a fine " Gothic " design (Fig. 68). Scott was very proud of the design and does not appear to have suffered from an inferiority complex, because he described it as " perhaps the best ever sent in to a competition, or nearly so." Then Lord Palmerston appeared on the scene and told Scott that he would have nothing to do with the Gothic style, and that it must be remodelled in the Italian manner, which he was quite sure Scott would be able to do very cleverly. Now " Pam " was Prime Minister and much more than a match for Scott, who in the end produced a new design, as Fig. 69. Now, whether this design is what Scott had in his mind when modernism passed away from him and every aspiration of his heart became medieval we cannot say. He seems to have been a little pleased with it, because in his " Recollections " he wrote : " My new designs were beautifully got up in outline ; the figures I put in myself and even composed the groups, for, though I have no skill in that way, I was so determined to show myself not behindhand with the Classicists that I seem to have more power than usual."

Mr. Harold Nicolson, in his book, " Curzon : The Last Phase," tells how Lord Curzon, when he took office as Secretary of State, on January 6th, 1919, paused at the doorway of the room in the Foreign Office in which he was to work and looked up at the cast-iron beams of its ceiling, disguised under an etrusco-byzantine stencilling, and exclaimed, " How ghastly—how positively ghastly ! "

Pam, however, had not administered a knock-out blow to Gothic, because Scott was to design the Albert Memorial in 1864, and St. Pancras Station, London, in 1866 ; and Street won the Law Courts, London, competition with a Gothic design in 1867. But these were the last, and in the end the Classic men won. From now on public buildings sprang up like mushrooms, and very terrible they were. A term " Free Classic " came into use. Columns, caps, architraves, friezes, cornices and pediments were heaped together in an architectural medley. It was freedom from all restraint. Certain vulgarians have described it as the " Undigested Architectural Vomit " style of design.

So at the beginning of our period you could still be Greek or Goth. There is a good tale told of a client who called on an architect then and complained that he had repeatedly said that the design he wanted must be Gothic, and all those sent to him were " Greek." " Well," said the architect, " I'm very sorry, but as a matter of fact my ' Gothic ' assistant is away ill."

HOUSES

Having noted this battle of the styles, we will now consider houses, and here we should like to mention, very honourably, the work of a man, George Devey, to whom we think sufficient importance is not paid to-day. Devey was born in 1820, and first wished to become a painter, and studied under John Sell Cotman. This early training turned him into a fine draughtsman with a good sense of

FIG. 70.—" Peacock " Tapestry. Designed by William Morris.
Produced by Morris & Co.

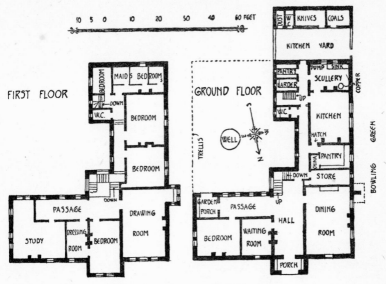

FIG. 71.—Plans of Red House.
(*Philip Webb, Architect*, 1859.)

colour. Why he turned to architecture we do not know, but in 1850 he was working at Penshurst. This wonderful fourteenth-century house, which we illustrated in Vol. II, must have influenced him. Fig. 77 shows the post office at Penshurst, which is dated 1850 on a plaster panel and was designed by Devey. This is very interesting indeed. Philip Webb and Norman Shaw were young men who had not started practice, and here was Devey doing work which clearly influenced Shaw in his early manner.

We can now pass to Red House, Bexley, Kent, which Philip Webb designed for William Morris. The contract was signed on May 16th, 1859, and William Kent was the builder. We have already dealt with the friendship of Webb and Morris in the " Cursory Chronicle " (p. 8), so no more need be said of how the house came to be built in an old apple orchard. The plan we show in Fig. 71, and the first thing which strikes one is that the aspect of the house had not been considered. People do not seem to have troubled about the sun ; in fact, they were rather

93

afraid of it. Complexions might suffer, or the carpets be faded. We know a school, built a little later, where all the classrooms were placed on the north side, and this is the case with the sitting-rooms at Red House, where the dining-room only catches a little afternoon sun; the south is wasted in passages, and the larder had sun on it till after twelve. There was no need for this, because the road is on the north, and nowadays all the rooms would have opened on to the garden to the south. There was no bathroom. Perhaps Morris used a shower bath, as Fig. 105, after the type shown by Leech in *Punch* in 1850; or hip-baths, as Fig. 106. In all other ways the house is well planned; the service between kitchen and dining-room is conveniently arranged.

Here is an interesting point. Devey, Webb and Shaw were to be responsible for bringing the kitchen up out of a dismal basement on to the ground-floor level. The Maidservants' League should put up a memorial to them in gratitude. Penshurst, built 1341, was far more sensibly planned for service to the dining-hall than the eighteenth-century Holkham we illustrated in Fig. 35, Vol. III. Here the kitchen was on the floor below the dining-room, and 180 feet away. The height of inconvenience was reached in one of Adams' villas—here the kitchen and offices interfered with the planning, so these were built at some distance from the house, in a pit dug in the ground, and screened with trees, and then connected by a subterranean passage with the basement of the villa. Princes seldom got their meat hot, or architects credit for their good intentions—but the nineteenth-century men did do some useful work in planning.

Red House was very well built, with external walls 1 foot 6 inches thick, and many 9-inch internal walls; there is enough brickwork to build three modern houses.

The original plans are in the Department of Engraving, Illustration and Design, at the Victoria and Albert Museum, South Kensington. We have prepared Fig. 71 from these,

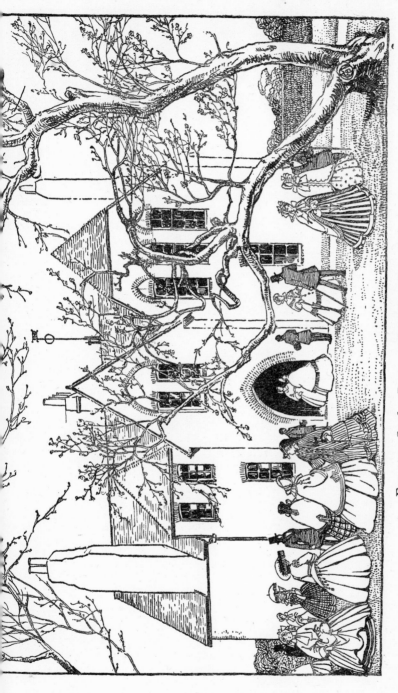

FIG. 72.—Garden Party at Red House in 1860.

Fig. 73.—Staircase, Red House.

(*Philip Webb, Architect,* 1859.)

96

Fig. 74.—" Evenlode " Chintz.   Designed by William Morris.
Produced by Morris & Co.

FIG. 75.—Dining-room Fireplace, Red House.
(*Philip Webb, Architect,* 1859.)

97

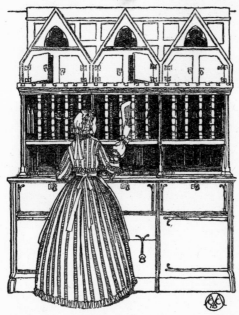

FIG. 76.—Dining-room Sideboard, Red House. (*Philip Webb, Architect*, 1859.)

and show on it the original uses of the rooms. There are as well two sketch plans for building a wing at the back, in quadrangular form, around the well. This was to house the Burne-Jones, who at one time thought of living with Morris.

The exterior, with its steeply-pitched roof, is very skilfully handled, with a touch of French feeling. Webb, like Morris, was a Goth, but that did not mean that he insisted on mullioned windows and lead glazing. He preferred sash windows as being more practical and modern, and so used these and grouped them together under arches. Here you have the beginnings of a modern architecture which, besides being good to look at, shall be comfortable to live in.

Figs. 73 and 75 show the treatment of the inside of the house. The brick fireplace in the dining-room must have been one of the first of this type used in modern houses. Brick-work exposed in this way was used in other parts of the house; there is an arch shown on the drawing of the oak staircase.

The furniture for the rooms must have presented great difficulties to Morris and Webb; antiques had not yet come into fashion, and in any case there were few antiques of their period. There was very little furniture in a fourteenth-century house such as Penshurst. We illustrated the tables

FIG. 77.—Group of Buildings by the Post Office at Penshurst, Kent.

(*George Devey, Architect,* 1850.)

[*Photo, W. Pollard.*

FIG. 78.—Red House, Bexley, Kent, designed for William Morris by Philip Webb and built 1859.

on trestles in the hall in Vol. II. The men sat on benches, with a very occasional chair of state, rather like a choir stall in a church. There were chests for keeping clothes in, bedsteads, cupboards, and not much else. So Webb had to invent the furniture for Red House, and most of this was coloured and decorated as Figs. 76, 79, 83 and 93. Beyond this were plans for frescoes on the walls. In the hall there was to be a great ship of Troy with the Greek heroes. Where the walls were not pain-

FIG. 79.—Hall Settle, Red House.
(*Philip Webb, Architect*, 1859.)

ted they were to be hung with tapestries, or printed cottons. What we have to remember is that the Morris group had never a good word to say for the Renaissance. To them it was a mere revival of paganism, and St. Paul's Cathedral, London, was a temple and not a Christian church. Morris loved colour and remembered—what we forget—that the mediæval church was all green and gold and red, with great frescoes on the walls of the lives of the saints. Eastern rugs were used on the floors, and rush-bottomed chairs for sitting on. The tables had plain oak tops which could be scrubbed, and these were set on trestles. Willow-

FIG. 80.—Glass Designed by Philip Webb, and blown by Powells.

pattern plates were used for the dinner service, and grey and blue Flanders ware for ornament. The table-glass was designed by Webb, and blown by Powells (Figs. 80 and 82).

Here we think Webb showed a fine appreciation of the wonderful craft of glass blowing. The glass is taken out of the furnace like a drop of liquid gold on the end of the long blowing tube. A good blow and this becomes a bubble—like blowing soap bubbles. If the bubble is held down its weight lengthens it to a sausage shape. If another blower with a little blob of glass on his blowpipe attaches this to the other end of the sausage, this can be drawn out into a long glass tube. But if the bubble, after being blown, is held upright, it flattens out into a bun shape. Pierce the top of the bun and whirl the bun shape, and the glass opens out into a flattened disc. This is how window glass used to be made, and the bull's-eye is where

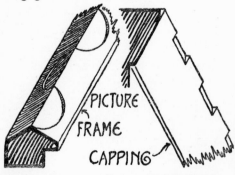

FIG. 81.—Woodwork Details (Philip Webb).

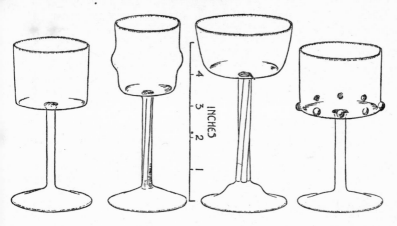

FIG. 82.—Glass Designed by Philip Webb and blown by Powells.

the disc was attached to the blowpipe. These are the movements possible to the blower, and beyond this he has only a shaping tool, rather like a pair of sugar tongs without the spoons at the end, and a stool with two arms projecting, on which he can roll his blowpipe and use the shaping tool on the glass. Glass-blowing is one of the most dexterous crafts we know of. Every boy and girl should see it done once, because it would show them what a wonderful thing the human hand is.

Red House is now in the occupation of Dr. A. H. Horsfall, and is being very well cared for.

We can now pass on to R. Norman Shaw (1831–1912), who, we saw on p. 26 followed Webb as Street's head assistant. Shaw had all the characteristics which go to make a

FIG. 83.—Desk Design by Philip Webb for Morris & Co.

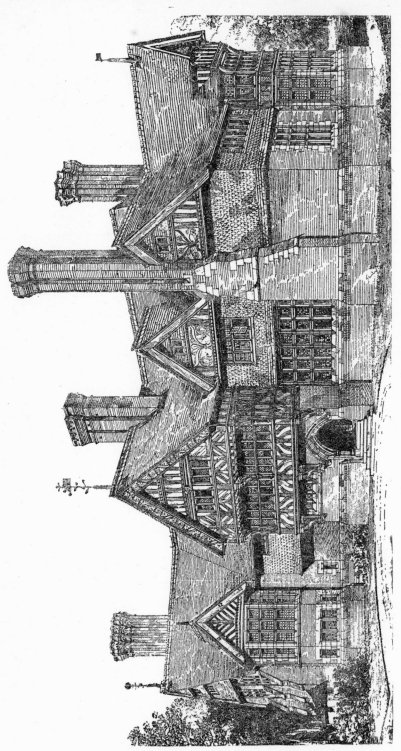

FIG. 84.—Grimsdyke, Harrow, 1872.

FIG. 85.—Rose and Lily Damask. By William Morris.
Produced by Morris & Co.

FIG. 86.—Study of a Lion.
[*From a sketch by Philip Webb in the possession of Messrs. Morris & Co., Ltd.*

Fig. 87.—The Seasons Tapestry. By William Morris. Produced by Morris & Co.

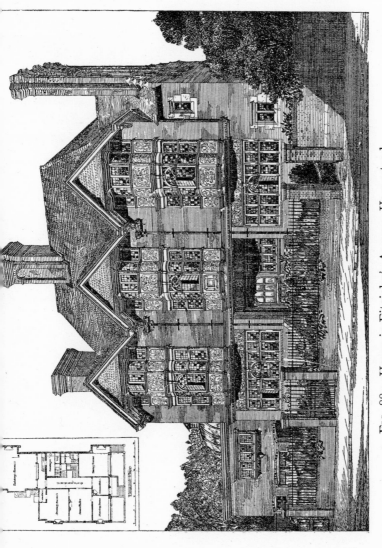

FIG. 88.—House in Fitzjohn's Avenue, Hampstead.

(From *Building News*, September 8th, 1882.)

(*Norman Shaw, Architect.*)

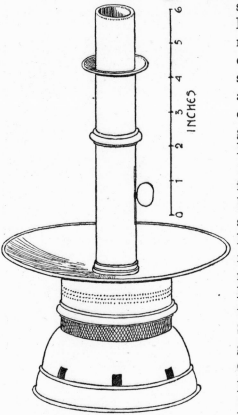

INCHES

FIG. 89.—Copper Candlestick belonging to Miss Walker. (Philip Webb.)

successful architect. He was a fine planner and a good draughtsman, possessed organizing ability, and a charm of manner which gained him clients. He shared offices in 1862 with Eden Nesfield, a brilliant man, but the partnership seems to have been a loose working arrangement which did not long continue. Designing at first in the Gothic manner, Shaw's houses were gabled and picturesque, with a great play of roofs. By 1874 he was building Lowther Lodge, now the home of the Royal Geographical Society, and in 1879 he was publishing the designs for a large house at Bedford Park for Mr. Carr, its proprietor. This latter work is very interesting, because it marks one of the first attempts by architects in our period of improving estate development. The general practice had been, and still is, for the speculating builder to buy some land, cut down all the trees, lay out the roads and then build as many stock pattern houses as possible.

Bedford Park seems to have been the private venture of Jonathan Carr, a London cloth merchant, who knew Morris and De Morgan. They may have recommended

FIG. 90.—An Air View of London's attractive Garden Suburb adjoining Hampstead Heath extension.

[*By courtesy of Aerofilms, Ltd.*]

FIG. 91.—No. 170 Queen's Gate, London.

(*R. Norman Shaw, Architect* 1888.)

FIG. 92.—No. 170 Queen's Gate, London.   The Hall.

(*R. Norman Shaw, Architect,* 1888.)

Shaw to him. E. J. May, to whom we are indebted for the information, was resident architect between 1880–90, and designed many houses there from Shaw's sketches, and, what is pleasant to relate, Shaw handed over the vicarage to May, "with his usual generosity," as his own job. Shaw himself did the club, church and Tabard Inn, and the large house for Carr.

FIG. 93.—Settle designed by Philip Webb for Morris & Co.

Shaw's work at Bedford Park, though of great interest, was not of such importance as Howard's later work at Letchworth. The first was just a pleasant oasis in the deserts of vulgarity ; the second something vital and new. Fig. 90 shows the interesting modern development of the Hampstead garden suburb, laid out from 1908 onwards.

Bedford Park is interesting as well because it marks the introduction of Early Renaissance detail, with nineteenth-century architectural design. This was wrongly called Queen Anne, and the sunflower was used for decoration. By 1888 Shaw was designing 170 Queens Gate (Figs. 91 and 92), near the Imperial Institute, South Kensington, which was built for Mr. White, of Portland Cement fame. Here you have sash windows, with a good cornice and a hipped roof. In fact, Shaw had arrived at the real Later Renaissance architecture, which we associate with Queen Anne and Sir Christopher Wren. We illustrate a superb

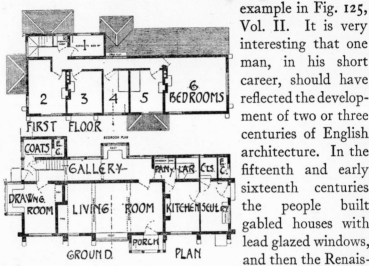

FIG. 94.—Plan of Cottage at Bishops Itchington.

(*C. F. A. Voysey, Architect.*)

example in Fig. 125, Vol. II. It is very interesting that one man, in his short career, should have reflected the development of two or three centuries of English architecture. In the fifteenth and early sixteenth centuries the people built gabled houses with lead glazed windows, and then the Renaissance came in, and they began to experiment with classic details and graft these on to Gothic forms. This was the Early Renaissance. Then Inigo Jones came back from Italy and designed the Banqueting Hall, in Whitehall, for James I in 1622. The Gothic form had disappeared and the building was completely classical, and later Wren's genius gave this type of design its distinctly and pleasantly English character. This was the Later Renaissance.

Shaw's Fig. 84 shows him as a Goth; Fig. 88 is Early Renaissance in character, and Fig. 91 distinctly Later Renaissance. The Renaissance was the rebirth of the old Roman classical architecture, and Rome borrowed from Greece—so you get back to Goth and Greek as the two original founts of inspiration. Shaw complained once to May that " he had spent years in persuading people to have mullioned windows with casements and lead glazing, and then he found it difficult to persuade them not to."

Mention should be made of the work of C. F. A. Voysey, who for some time was an assistant of George Devey, of whom we have already written. Fig. 95 shows one of the

Fig. 95.—Cottage at Bishops Itchington, Warwick (1889).
(*C. F. A. Voysey, Architect.*)

first houses designed by Mr. Voysey as early as 1889. This
has a remarkably modern quality and, like his later work,
has not dated itself. To illustrate how prices have increased,
the house was built for £559. C. R. Macintosh, who
designed the Glasgow School of Art in 1894, and George
Walton, who did the early Kodak shops in London, can
be instanced as other pioneers in the modern movement,
and Edgar Wood was another.

Space precludes us following up the development of
domestic architecture, though some post first war examples
are given in Chapter IV, and really there was no very considerable development between 1890 and 1914. You could
be Goth or Greek, and it is amazing how the Gothic forms
persist, and how people love gabled houses. We heard an
amusing tale of an elderly architect who was commissioned
by his brother to design a house in 1931. The elderly
architect had noticed that the younger men were designing
houses with flat roofs, and hailed the commission as an
opportunity to follow suit and "go modern" at the

FIG. 96.—Mahogany Sofa, covered with horsehair, made for
Mary Bulmer, aged three, in 1851.
(*Bethnal Green Museum, London.*)

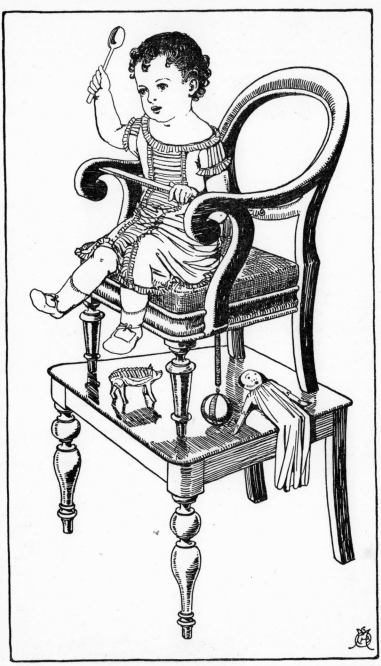

FIG. 97.—Mahogany High Chair, seat covered with Horsehair,
about 1860.
(*Bethnal Green Museum, London.*)

FIG. 98.—Table in English Oak. (Gimson.)

expense of his brother; but the latter proved very intractable and was horrified. "Flat roofs in Sussex," he exclaimed. "Nonsense. I want some good oak, and gables, and lead glazing." The elderly architect wept buckets; he pointed out that lead glazing was invented when glass was very expensive, and so it was sound economy to use up small pieces by leading them together, but now that you could obtain large sheets these should be used. "If you were logical," he exclaimed, the tears coursing down his cheeks, "you would glaze the windscreen of your car with lead glazing, frame up its body with good English oak, and plaster the panels in wattle and daub." But tears availed him not—in Sussex!

Now the reason for this is racial and psychological. The Englishmen are descended from certain hairy barbarians who descended on our coasts in A.D. 449, and these Angles, Saxons and Jutes came from outside the old Roman Empire. They had not absorbed the Greek culture and their descendants are much

FIG. 99.—Wardrobe. (Ambrose Heal, 1897.)

the same; they make a mess of their towns, have not learned to plan, have no idea of order, and remain good Goths. They prefer persons to plans.

FIG. 100.—The " Dryad " Chair (1908).

FURNITURE

We have already illustrated some of Webb's furniture (Figs. 76, 79, 83 and 93), done in connection with Morris. That was one school — the school of the insurgents, who would have nothing to do with the world as it was. By the kindness of Radio Pictures Ltd., we are enabled to publish a photograph from that admirable film, " Little Women " (Fig. 107), which shows how ordinary nice people furnished their homes in America in the time of the Civil War (c. 1860). Though the furniture was not beautiful, they achieved a certain

FIG. 101.—6-in. De Morgan Tile.

FIG. 102.—*L'Art Nouveau.*
(*Bethnal Green Museum*)

solid comfort. We enjoyed this film more than any we have seen for a long time. It seemed to us a real contribution to history with its carefully considered backgrounds, against which moved the four little women, with that genius, Katharine Hepburn, as " Jo."

Figs. 96 and 97 show two amusing pieces from the Bethnal Green Museum, London. The child's couch shows the end of Greek detail in furniture design, and the baby's high chair is a very heavy, cumbersome thing for a baby. The chair was fixed to the table under it by a rod and thumbscrew, and this being unscrewed, the chair was placed at the side of the table for the infant to play with its toys, which were sometimes carved in wood, as Figs. 103 and 104. This kind of furniture followed all the architectural fashions until the 'eighties, when, under the guidance of Norman Shaw, the people began to turn back to antiques, and Chippendale, Hepplewhite and Sheraton came into their own once more. As the available quantity of real antiques was limited, the faker got to work and these were reproduced.

But the insurgent school continued, and foremost among

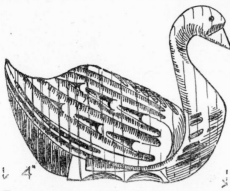

FIG. 103.—Carved Wooden Toy Animal.

them was Ernest Gimson, an architect, who, born in 1864, came to London, fell under the influence of Morris, so that he forsook his profession, and went to the Cotswolds to practise the crafts. There he built the most beautiful cottages of the local stone, and made furniture as Fig. 98, and generally enjoyed himself—but it was all a great mistake, because Gimson was a very gifted man who, instead of playing at peasant art, should have been trying to improve the work of his own time.

By about 1897 Ambrose Heal was designing plain oak furniture (Fig. 99) for those people who wished to live the simple life, and Heal, having a shop of his own, was able to influence the furnishing trade very considerably—and there were many others.

Another amusing revival was that of cane furniture. Mr. B. J. Fletcher, Principal of the Leicester School of Art, brought back a chair from Austria, and started making them in his school. From this grew the Dryad Cane Furniture Works, which started in 1907, and Fig. 100 shows a "Dryad" chair which we bought soon after

FIG. 104.—Carved Wooden Toy Animal.

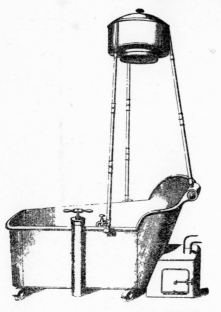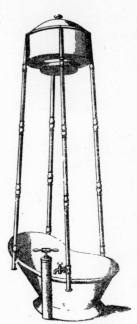

FIG. 105.—Baths (1855–60) from a contemporary Catalogue of
George Jennings (Lambeth).

—as it is still in use it speaks well for Dryad
work.

By this time the insurgents had worn themselves out,
and the simple-lifers had found that their simplicity was
really an extreme form of sophistication—then an extraordinary thing happened. The Continental people discovered Morris, and at the 1900 Paris Exhibition *L'Art
Nouveau* appeared, as Fig. 102; several other pieces can
be seen at Bethnal Green. This had no following in
England, where the designers remained contented with
reproductions and slight variants. Out of *L'Art Nouveau*,
however, much better things were done on the Continent,
and probably the good work in Sweden to-day could be
traced back to Morris and Webb.

SPECIAL BUILDINGS, BATHS AND WASH-HOUSES

We are afraid that when the time comes for us all to
be dug up, say, about A.D. 3000, the archæologists of that

period will not pay very much attention to the few houses designed by the architects. The Evans and Bulleids of that day will come across these, and dismiss them as not being representative. The square miles of suburban development done by the speculating builder in the nineteenth century, without any architect (Fig. 59), will be held to be typical of the period, and learned papers will be read on the subject.

FIG. 106.—The Hip Bath.

The architects, however, who will come into their own will be those men who designed all the special buildings which were built to meet the new needs which arose in the nineteenth century. In the old days a few hundred years could go to the evolution of buildings; in the nineteenth century entirely new types had to be evolved at once. The architects who did this were seldom knighted, and the Royal Academy did not admit them to its ranks, but they were the men who were doing the really useful and most difficult work.

We will take baths and wash-houses. We have seen in Vol. III what grubby people the early industrialists were, and how the workers lived in back-to-back houses, without any conveniences at all, and day by day they got grubbier and grubbier. Something had to be done about it. Cleanliness is next to Godliness, but the industrial town was an ungodly invention—so the industrialists turned to cleanliness, and on August 26th, 1846, an Act was passed " to Encourage the Establishment of Public Baths and Washhouses." The preamble stated that " Whereas it is desirable for the Health, Comfort and Welfare of the Inhabitants of Towns and populous Districts to encourage the Establishment therein of Public Baths and Washhouses and open Bathing Places ; be it enacted by the Queen's most Excellent Majesty," etc. In consequence of this Act councils were allowed to borrow money to build baths, and make charges for their use ; so the bath, which had been a common feature of Roman Britain, came into being once more.

Instead of illustrating one of the earliest types, we have chosen one of the quite recent : the Westminster Public Baths, at Marshall Street, London, opened in 1931 (Fig. 108). This is the headquarters of the Amateur Diving Association, and various championships are held there, including Oxford and Cambridge University swimming, and the arrangement of seating for spectators is the right one. The Westminster baths were designed by A. W. S. and K. M. B. Cross, who are specialists in this kind of work.

Let us turn to the actual planning of the baths as shown in Fig. 109. Messrs. Cross had to provide, not only a first-class swimming bath, but a second-class one as well. These had first to be of the sizes which are required by the Amateur Swimming Association, and of depths sufficient for diving. The entrances had to be so arranged that the bather could not only undress but cleanse himself before entering the actual bath ; a very necessary precaution for men whose work during the day is dirty. All this is complicated by the fact that mixed bathing is allowed, so that separate dressing-rooms must be provided. Had Messrs. Cross only had to provide these two swimming baths their task would have been comparatively simple. In addition, however, they had to arrange for a public wash-house, where poor people could bring their clothes in prams to be

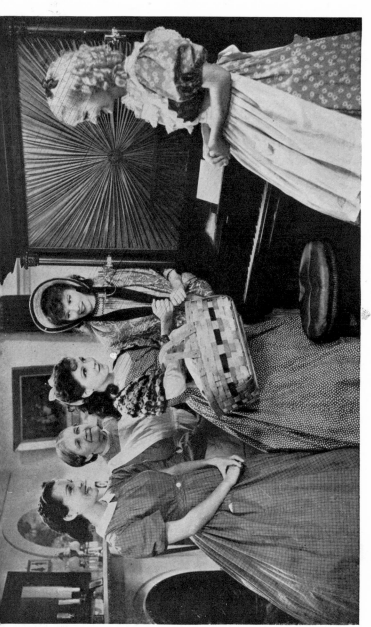

FIG. 107.—The "Little Women" and Hannah.

[From the film, by the courtesy of Radio Pictures Ltd.

FIG. 108.—First-class Swimming Bath, Marshall Street Baths, London.

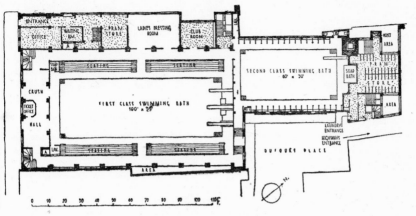

FIG. 109.—Plan of Marshall Street Baths, London.
(A. W. S. and K. M. B. Cross, Architects.)
(R.I.B.A. Journal, January, 1934.)

washed. Fig. 109 shows the pram store at the end of the building. On the floors above this is a large laundry with washing machines, drying horses and a mangling room. This was not all, because there are first and second-class slipper baths, for men and women, over the crush hall and all that part of the plan above the first-class swimming bath in Fig. 108. A slipper bath is just an ordinary bath in a little cubicle, about 6 feet by 7 feet, where people who have not baths in their own houses can enjoy one for a few pence. All these

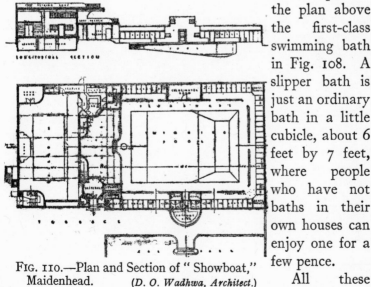

FIG. 110.—Plan and Section of "Showboat,"
Maidenhead. *(D. O. Wadhwa, Architect.)*

parts of the building must be kept separate. It would not do at all if an old lady, pushing her pram full of washing to the laundry, found her way into a diving competition instead. Each part has its own separate entrance and staircases and sanitary accommodation and fire escape. Then there is all the enormous complication of plumbing to be thought of ; baths must be filled and emptied, and so on. The Westminster Baths are just off Regent Street, and should be visited by anyone interested in the subject.

We close this section with a view and plan of the "Showboat," at Maidenhead (Figs. 110 and 111), designed by D. C. Wadhwa, and a very pleasant example of one of the roadhouses which have become popular since the first war. Here the architecture is very good indeed. The plan (Fig. 110) is a straightforward one, and the elevations are the result of the construction—the design is functional, and surely infinitely better than anything of the fake nature of "Ye Olde Tea Shoppe."

We have seen that baths were beginning to be used more generally in private houses. Thackeray wrote in " Pendennis " of shower baths, and one of these, which had been presented to the poet Burns, was sold when his wife died in 1834.

CHURCHES

With churches you could be Greek or Goth, so we will start with " Greek " Thomson, who was born in 1817 and did most of his work in Glasgow. He never went to Greece, but appears to have saturated himself with Greek detail ; hence the prefix. Fig. 113 shows the Caledonia Road Church, in Glasgow, designed by Thomson, and it is a striking composition; the memorial stone was laid on April 29th, 1856, and the church opened on March 22nd, 1857. It is founded on the Erechtheum at Athens, illustrated in our book on Classical Greece, and which was used as well by Inwood at St. Pancras Church, London, in 1819,

FIG. III.—A typical Open-air Pool at a Roadhouse: " Showboat," Maidenhead.
(*D. G. Wadhwa, Architect.*)

[*R.I.B.A. Journal,* Jan., 1934.]

FIG. 112.—Interior of St. Agnes' Church, Kennington, London.
(George Gilbert Scott, Jnr., Architect, 1875.*)*

FIG. 113.—Caledonia Road Church, Glasgow.
(" *Greek* " *Thomson, Architect,* 1856.)

and by many other architects since. A very hopeless proceeding this—to take a marble portico from the sunny city and blue skies of Athens and stick it up in the grey air of Glasgow—but a difficult one to do as well as Thomson did. Here we see the end of the work which started with the publication of Stuart and Revett's "Antiquities of Athens" in 1762, and finished in England with the work of Cockerell and Elmes.

This church of Thomson's enables us to fire off a little squib of our own. From time to time one hears of discussions as to whether the Classics should continue to be taught, and by Classics are meant the masterpieces of Greek and Roman literature. Now whether it does anybody any good to struggle with the grammar and syntax of these ancient tongues we cannot say ; a few may obtain sufficient mastery, but for the many it is casting pearls before porkers. What we do say—and that without any fear of contradiction—is that no one can understand English architecture unless they know something of Greek and Roman everyday life and things.

Now we can return to the Gothic churches which had been built by Pugin, Scott, Butterfield and Street. As a result of the Oxford Revival of 1833, Gothic had become fashionable for churches once more, and there is much to be said for it, if only the spirit of Gothic could be caught and carried on. The idea can be tested on any day by paying a visit to Westminster Abbey and St. Paul's Cathedral and deciding which is the better of the two for worship. The Revivalists decided on the Abbey, but they missed the point that the real Gothic architecture was a continuous growth—that one century did not copy another. This is what the Revivalists did ; they proceeded to try and work in exact Gothic design, preferably of the Early English or Early Decorated. At first they wanted as well to get their churches rather on the cheap, so poor, thin, lifeless buildings arose in the dreary wastes of nineteenth-century suburbs, and somehow or other these did not suggest that

GOTHIC

they had been built to the glory of God. Then an architect
of genius appeared in the person of George Gilbert Scott,
jun., the son of Sir Gilbert, and his architecture was a
very different kind of work from the father's. Fig. 112
shows the interior of St. Agnes', Kennington, in South
London, which was first published in the *Building News*
of July 16th, 1875. When this appeared it caused a furore
among the architects, and they were not at all pleased with
it, so Mr. Walter Millard tells us. St. Agnes' was not
thirteenth century; if anything it seemed to be based
on Decorated or fourteenth-century work. Letters appeared in the architectural Press about the outrage. One
man regretted that there had been no description of the
church in the *Building News*, but added: " Your readers
will agree that any description would be superfluous. The
less said about such a thing the better." Another corre-
spondent replied that his office boy had been so charmed
with the plate that he had stolen it. J. D. Sedding entered
the lists, and said that St. Agnes'was a fine design, as it is.
In the end it marked some departure from the stylists and
proved the inspiration of many a modern church, and perhaps of the cathedral at Liverpool, the competition for
which was won, in 1903, by Giles Gilbert, the third generation of the Scott architects. But whether it is possible to
produce Gothic architecture in the twentieth century we
should not care to say. The real stuff was the reflection of a
mode of living entirely different from our own. Life in the
Middle Ages was based on co-operation; ours turns to
competition and profit. This is really a test question:
Can a commercial community build a church to the Glory
of God, and if so, how ?

St. Agnes', however, is very well worth a visit, and it
is only about 1d. fare in a tram from Westminster Bridge
to Kennington Park. At the entrance to this are the
cottages Prince Albert built after the 1851 Exhibition,
which we illustrated in Vol. III. St. Agnes' stands at the
back of the Park, and on the east side is a house built for

the Bishop of Rochester by Norman Shaw. The neighbourhood is a dismal one now, but nice old Regency houses do remain, and all can be seen in one morning.

SCHOOLS

The nineteenth-century industrialists treated children badly. Something very much like slavery existed, because by reason of the low wages paid to the parents the children were driven into the factories and mines in the desperate attempt to obtain sufficient food. Infant paupers were sold into bondage willy-nilly. Very little could be done for their education ; still attempts were being made. Sunday schools were established at Gloucester in 1783, and these played their part in education. Farington, the painter, noted how in 1801 he saw children coming out of a mill at Cranford at seven in the evening, and they had been at work since six or seven in the morning. These children attended church morning and afternoon one Sunday, and school the next. However, something was being done for the education of the working children, even if it was at the expense of their day of rest. There were many kinds of schools, of course, from the great public school downwards, and many private schools, again downwards, until you got to the Do-the-Boys-Hall which Dickens satirized in " Nicholas Nickleby," and little dame schools. At the beginning of the nineteenth century the Dissenters and Quakers were interesting themselves in education and founding schools.

Soon after this, in 1811, the National Society for Promoting the Education of the Children of the Poor in the Principles of the Established Faith was founded. But it was not obligatory that children must attend the schools, and the church school was more generally built in the villages and country than in the industrial town.

So long as Industrialism claimed the bodies of the poorer children they could not go to school ; in many places there were no schools to go to. But the Government began to realize that something must be done and started giving grants to schools in 1833.

But Industrialism continued to develop on the sweated labour of man, woman and child, until a champion arose in the person of the Earl of Shaftesbury. Under the 1833 Act the labour of children under thirteen was limited to eight hours a day, and between thirteen and eighteen not more than sixty-nine hours weekly. This was above ground in mills, and the manufacturers foretold that they would be ruined and unable to compete in world markets without child labour.

So things went on until the publication of the Report of the Royal Commission on Mines, 1842, drew attention to conditions of labour underground. This led to an Act which prohibited the employment of women and girls underground in mines altogether, and of boys under ten. Previous to this it was quite usual for boys of seven to be sent into the mines.

Gradually Lord Shaftesbury and his friends delivered the children from bondage, and so we come to the introduction of the Education Act of 1870 by W. E. Forster, which provided for public elementary education in England and Wales. This, though it was obligatory, was not free ; the parents paid a small fee. The public elected School Boards to carry out the Act, hence the schools they built were called Board Schools. Edward R. Robson, F.R.I.B.A., was appointed architect to the School Board for London, and he must be accounted one of the men who did fine, useful work. First he went on a tour of inspection of schools in Belgium, Germany, Austria, Switzerland and France, in 1873, and his book on " School Architecture," which we note in our List of Authorities, summarized the results of his tour.

This tour of Robson's was very necessary, because there were no buildings in England which could be taken as models for board schools to accommodate perhaps 1000

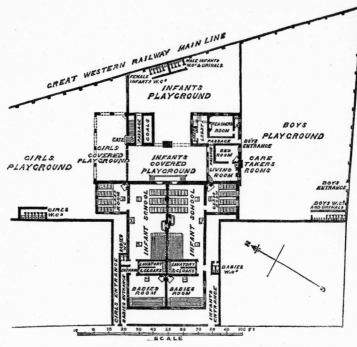

FIG. 114.—Ground Plan of Wornington Road School.

children. In Germany and Holland, Robson found that not

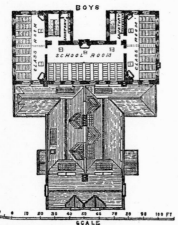

FIG. 115.—First and Second Floor Plans of Wornington Road School.

only had all teachers to be qualified, but all buildings suitable for teaching, though one difficulty was that in Germany, for example, the separate teacher and class-room was the rule, while in England it was the exception in 1870. This fundamental difference influenced the planning of schools, and reflects more credit on Robson in that he could only benefit by the detail observed during his tour and had to invent the

124

Fig. 116.—Wornington Road Board School, N.W. London.

(From "School Architecture," 1877.) (E. R. Robson, Architect.)

125

general plan himself. To him more than any other man must be given the credit of having evolved the Board School plan; and it was a tremendous work. In London alone it was reckoned that as a result of the 1870 Act school accommodation for 112,000 children would have to be provided; and the Act covered England and Wales.

The crux of the problem of education in England was first the monitor, and then, after 1846, the pupil teacher. This meant that the schools had to be planned with large schoolrooms, under the control of a master, assisted by a pupil teacher, with only a few separate classrooms. The pupil teacher was a scholar who at fourteen was apprenticed for five years in the school, just as in a trade. They continued their own education and had to pass examinations until they became certificated, and certainly learned their job in a practical way. As well that the pupils benefited by a " sympathy of numbers," but the schoolrooms must have been noisy.

The elementary schools of 1870 were divided into six grades, or standards, above the infants, and the Board of Education laid down in their code that a certificated teacher could teach sixty pupils, assisted by a pupil teacher, and for every additional forty another pupil teacher could be added, and for every additional eighty either one more teacher or two pupil teachers. Classes of eighty were held to be possible, if taught by one teacher and pupil teacher together.

It was these conditions which settled the plans of the early board schools, and we publish one of these in Fig. 116, of the Wornington Road School, in the north-west of London. Fig. 114 shows the ground plan of the building, and Fig. 115 the first and second floors. Taking the ground floor first, Robson arranged that the girls' and infants' entrances were side by side, so that the big girls could bring their infant brothers and sisters to school. Boys, being of a rough and turbulent nature, had their own entrance some way away. Then the playgrounds all had to be schemed on a rather irregular site, and separate staircases up to the boys' department on the first floor, and the girls' on the second. Fig. 116 shows how all these parts were contrived to form one pleasant-looking building; 492 infants, 306 boys and 318 girls were accommodated in it, at a cost of £1870 for the land and £7845 for the building.

When you consider that the board school had to be invented we think our readers will agree that the work was very well done indeed. One amusing detail is given by Robson. The new board schools were built in the slums, but the people were not at all grateful; in fact, they rose up in their wrath at this interference with their liberty. To be forced to send their children to school was too much so they chased away the unfortunate builders, who had to be given police protection while building.

We have detailed the advance made in secondary education for girls on p. 15. It must be remembered, however, that, after elementary schools had been begun, secondary schools followed, and an endless variety of technical schools and colleges, and the post first world-war years have seen the erection of a great number of these institutions, of many kinds, but almost always of imposing size.

The last ten or fifteen years have witnessed some marked changes in school planning, which have spread the accommodation over a wide one-storey area, with classrooms spaced about and projecting to catch more light and air; the very antithesis, in fact, of the old several-storey Board School with central hall and surrounding classrooms. Incidentally it is noteworthy that many schools during the second great war removed to large country houses, after the first and most painful example of Malvern College to Blenheim Palace. One south coast preparatory school found itself in a fully moated fifteenth-century West Country house. They squeezed the scholars into the old building for bed and board, but had to adapt the stable court for teaching purposes.

CHAPTER IV

POST-FIRST-GREAT-WAR PROBLEMS AND CONSTRUCTION

IN every age there are certain irascible old gentlemen who shake their heads and say that people are going to the dogs—especially the young people. To-day they do actually go to the dogs, to see them race, but this is not what the ancients mean. They mean that the young people will make experiments ; they produce stark-looking houses paintings which do not follow the accepted standard, and sculptures not founded on Greek models, and so the old men are shocked and tend to become explosive. It may be worth while to examine this a little, because it is not only a question of external design, but the reflection of something inward and spiritual.

Looking back, we remember our own youth as safe and secure. If you gave the impression that you were conducting your affairs so that your life was following, approximately, the lines laid down by the industrious apprentice, then you might look for some measure of success. To-day this is not so. There is not enough work to go round, and young men and women do not feel secure. They feel that the world has failed them, and so are not prepared to follow the old standards, but are seeking to set up new ones of their own. All this is reflected in the arts, and it is healthy and stimulating.

Take painting. We went some little while ago to an exhibition of students' work at a well-known art school, where we knew the principal. There were oil studies of the figure there which appeared to be made up of cylindrical forms of various sizes, in green, and purple, and black, painted by quite nice young girls. We remembered the

Whistler tale of the man who, confronted by the nineteenth-century parallel of this, said, "Well, I can't see anything in this"; to which Whistler replied, "Don't you wish you could?" So we condemned ourselves as old-fashioned and passed on to the sculpture. But here we were equally at fault. Form seemed to be reproduced on the lines of the common household loaf and was blobular, or strangely geometrical.

When we come to post-war building, however, we feel on safer ground, and the starkness seems both purposeful and proper; there is something very honest about it. Any building which stands up must have an honest foundation and be well constructed, or it would fall down. You may design castles in the air, but they must be built on the solid ground. So we will examine the constructional side of building first.

If we begin with the houses in the Middle Ages, these were rather like barns, and the barns, with aisles at each side, were like churches. Figs. 83 and 113 in Vol. I illustrate this type of construction. If you wanted more room you made gabled ends on to the main roof, until you got to the ⊓ plan of Elizabethan times. The roof was a very essential part of planning; the builder always had to consider this and to provide good walls to carry it.

This remained until well on in the eighteenth century. Wren's houses always had a good roof to them. We showed this type in A and B, Fig. 33, Vol. III. At the end of the century, when the attics, which had been in the roof, were given walls of their own, as F, Fig. 33, Vol. III, the actual roof disappeared behind parapet walls and ceased to have much significance, until it was revived again by Webb and Shaw as shown by Figs. 78, 84 and 88 in this book. But roofs had never been so troublesome to builders as floors.

If we turn back to the floor over the great hall of the Norman keep we illustrated in Fig. 7, Vol. I, the problem here was to cover a space 31 feet 6 inches by 40 feet. Had the Norman builders determined to bridge across the

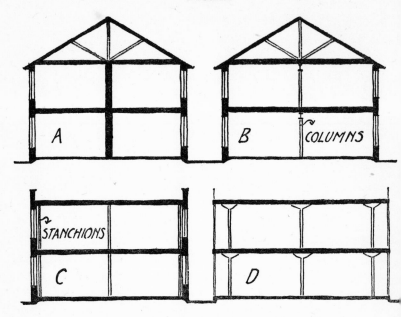

FIG. 117.—Evolution of Steel-framed Building.

narrower span they would have had to find oak beams, say, 34 feet long; a difficult matter. Instead they threw a great stone arch across the hall, 3 feet thick, and used this to pick up the ends of smaller beams placed longways. The arch was not constructed ornament, but ornamental construction.

If we turn to A, Fig. 117, we shall find that the late eighteenth-century builder was not much better off for materials than the twelfth-century builder of Castle Hedingham; he had to have a good many walls inside his buildings to carry the floors. This had not mattered when he was building houses, because he could span the floors of any room in wood; or if, for example, he was building an assembly hall, then the floor of this could be carried on the walls of smaller rooms under. There would only be the one large hall in the building. With the advent of Industrialism, however, factories and mills had to be designed with large open spaces on each floor, and the floors had to be strong enough to carry heavy machinery.

According to " Modern Steelwork," published by the British Steelwork Association, it was in 1801 that " cast-iron floor beams, to the design of James Watt (1736–1819), were used in a Manchester cotton mill. This is the first instance on record of the successful use of cast iron for floor beams." If this is so, Watt not only perfected the steam engine in 1781, which brought the factory system into being, but can be taken as the father of our own very up-to-date post-war steel-framed buildings with flat roofs.

Cast iron had already been used for other forms of structural work. We illustrated the famous Coalbrookdale Bridge in Vol. III, Fig. 74, erected in 1779, with a span of 100 feet. The Menai Bridge was opened in 1826. Professor A. E. Richardson has kindly provided us with the details of cast-iron girders, as Fig. 118, which he discovered when carrying out alterations at University College, London. These span over a void of 40 feet, the rest of the construction being in timber, and were used by Wilkins, the architect, in 1827. Another cast-iron girder used in railway construction about 1833 can still be seen over an archway near Berkhamsted Station, on the L.M.S. Railway.

By 1832 a beginning was made in the use of *wrought iron* for girder construction. The 1851 Exhibition building, which became the Crystal Palace, was a combination of cast-iron columns with wrought-iron bracings and roof trusses, and in 1856 Bessemer announced his method of *steel* conversion. The time was now ripe for revolutionary happenings in construction, yet just at this time Devey, Webb and Shaw were planning and carrying out a revival of the old methods.

We can now trace the evolution of steel construction in Fig. 117. A shows how, up till the end of the eighteenth century, the internal wall played its part in carrying the floors. In B can be seen the application of Watt's cast-iron

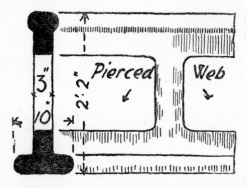

FIG. 118.—Cast-iron Girder, University College, London.
(*Wilkins, Architect*, 1827.)

girder, placed longitudinally and supported by cast-iron columns, and on to which the transverse wooden joists could bear, but the external walls still remained and were really structural. Such a mill, dating from 1835, is shown in Fig. 141, Vol. III.

These external walls presented the next difficulty, because light was very essential; but if the windows were made too wide, not sufficient brickwork was left to carry the floors with their load of machinery, so good piers of brickwork were provided here, rather like the buttresses of a church wall; but these cut off light. Then iron or steel stanchions were used instead, as at C, and by now the external walls were not doing very much more than support themselves.

The next development came with the completely steel-framed building, as Fig. 119. Here all the floors and roof were carried by steel, and the outside walls had ceased to function. In fact, windows and quite thin outer partitions to keep out the weather were all that was necessary to turn the structure into a habitable building. It was rather like a mediæval timber-framed building, where the external filling-in was carried out in wattle and daub. It was a sad day for the architects and the clients who demanded a proper proportion of columns, pilasters, cornices, pediments and all the paraphernalia to which they were used, and which once had been structural and useful. So these continued to be used, and are still, but it is the steel frame which is doing the work. Many modern buildings are constructional inexactitudes.

FIG. 119.—55 Broadway, Westminster, London.
The Building on September 8th, 1928.
(*Adams, Holden and Pearson, Architects.   J. R. Sharman, Engineer.*)

Fig. 120.—The Passenger Transport Board Offices at 55 Broadway, Westminster, London.

(*Adams, Holden and Pearson, Architects.*)

[*By courtesy of the London Passenger Transport Board.*

LIGHT

Some few men, however, have cut themselves away from traditional treatment, and are boldly adventuring with the new methods of construction. Fig. 119, of 55 Broadway, Westminster, the Passenger Transport Board offices in London, seems to us a fine example. Here the steel frame has been sheathed with stone, and the building expresses itself rather by its shape than by added and unnecessary architectural detail. Fig. 119 shows the steel frame being erected in 1928, and Fig. 120 is of the completed building. This should be visited—and carefully examined. The plan is extraordinarily skilful, and the construction a splendid example, when you discover that it has been built on the top of an underground railway. The building is decorated with some modern sculpture which is rather beyond us. Messrs. Adams, Holden and Pearson were the architects, and J. R. Sharman the engineer.

D, Fig. 117, shows a further logical building development. Where great light is desired it is quite possible to cantilever the floors out beyond the last line of floor supports, so that the outer casing can, if need be, be constructed wholly of glass as Fig. 132. You can, if you so desire, turn a part of your house into a great solarium. That is an interesting detail. We saw on p. 93 that, when Webb designed Red House for Morris, they did not worry much about the sun; to-day we all crave for the sun, light and air.

So that we have arrived at this position. The external walls and roof have ceased to have their old significance. In the modern building it is the floor and its supports which are structural, and, freed from the bondage of the roof, the floors can be of any shape you like. Your plan could be swept round in a great curve, as Fig. 128, or follow some geometrical shape if desired, and the flat roof adds so much extra space economically and can be used. Flat roofs then are not fads, but the logical outcome of the constructional evolution we have been describing. The modern steel-framed building is in reality a revival of one

CONCRETE

of the very oldest building methods. It would be quite easy to link up 55 Broadway (Fig. 120) and Stonehenge. Both are post and lintel construction. If you can imagine, say, twelve Stonehenges built one on top of the other, that would be a stone-framed building; modern builders do the same thing in steel.

Reinforced concrete must be mentioned as another modern constructional development. This seems to have been started by a French market gardener, Monier by name, who made some flower tubs with cement and reinforced them with metal. He was so pleased with the result that he patented the idea in 1867. To-day we not only make tubs, but fencing posts, piles and poles in concrete, and many other things. Hennebique and Coignet were two French pioneers who carried out fine engineering works in the method in the 'nineties, but it has not been so much used here as the steel frame. Reinforced concrete is an entirely novel way of construction; the carpenter makes the moulds into which the concrete is cast, and this adds to the cost. But its flexibility and wide range of use are amazing.

As to houses—let us see how these have come into being during our period. Many attempts have been made to improve the all-pervading, useful, but unimaginative speculative building. Norman Shaw and E. J. May were working in this way at Bedford Park, 1880-90. William Willett, of Daylight Saving fame, and G. W. Hart, of Hampstead, were good speculating builders, who employed architects to design their houses. The speculating builder scored heavily in the direction of economy, because he could standardise the building of his houses, and there is no harm in standardization; in fact, it is necessary. Wren's houses were standardized. These all had the same kind of windows, doors and architectural details. You can say that the period of this book is the only one in which all the people have agreed to differ architecturally. Fig. 61 reflects this, and from a manufacturing point of view it is

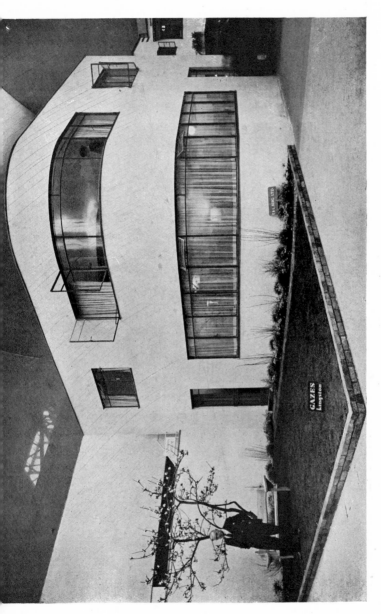

Fig. 121.—" Sunspan " House exhibited at Olympia, London, in 1934.
(*Wells Coates and Pleydell-Bouverie, Architects.*)

Fig. 122.—" Sunspan " House.   The principal Bedroom.

Fig. 123.—" Sunspan " House.   The Living-room.

(Wells Coates and Pleydell-Bouverie, Architects.)

ridiculous ; think of cars produced in this fashion.

In the year 1934 certain young archi-tects suggested a more rational course. Figs. 121–125 show the "Sunspan" House which was built and exhibited in the Ideal Home Exhibition at Olym-pia. There are a number of models, just like a motor-car. You can select a week-end cottage, or a larger house with

FIG. 124.—The Lay-out of a Group of "Sunspan" Houses.
(*Wells Coates and Pleydell-Bouverie, Architects.*)

five bedrooms, or one with four or three.

Inside the house other revolutions have been going on. The Victorian sitting-room was rather like a junk shop, with innumerable objects which had to be dusted day after day, and at which nobody glanced once in a blue moon. " Away with them," say the young designers ; " we will have everything glittering and clean." So they are ex-perimenting with chromium steel, glass and cellulose paint, and their furniture is fitted in as part of the fabric. Fig. 127 shows how good their kitchens are.

People have forgotten how uncomfortable the Victorians were. They sat in their straight-backed chairs in rooms which were only heated by fog-producing coal fires and lit by air-consuming fish-tail gas burners. Their bedrooms were arctic in the winter, and the only hot water was that pro-duced by the boiler at the back of the kitchen range. A bath was a once-a-week luxury. Refrigeration was unheard of, and the butter ran on the plate in the summer. The

K 135

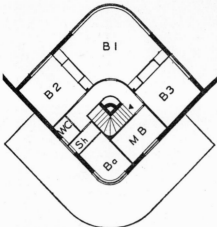

FIRST FLOOR PLAN

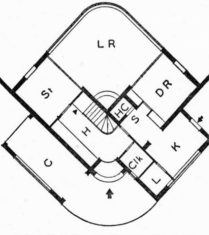

GROUND FLOOR PLAN

FIG. 125.—Plan of "Sunspan" House.

housemaids sprinkled tea-leaves on the floor when they swept it, but the dust rose and settled on the furniture —there were no vacuum cleaners to take it away.

Fig. 126 shows one of the studios of the B.B.C. at Birmingham, by Serge Chermayeff—and a very pleasant interior it is with its modern furniture—Fig. 128 a departmental store, and Fig. 129 the L.M.S. Hotel at Morecambe.

From time to time we have welcomed distinguished artists to our shores, with great benefit to ourselves. Recently Erich Mendelsohn has come to live here, and it is with the greatest pleasure we include one of his designs in Fig. 128.

The war of 1939 has, for the time, rendered what has been written about houses of glass for sunlight the dream mirage of a vanished world. Just as the restriction of imports has set us back for years in our dietary, so for the first time for 500 years Englishmen have had to take urgent thought for defence in their homes. The only war-time housing is for munition or industrial work, and for this the Royal Institute of British Architects

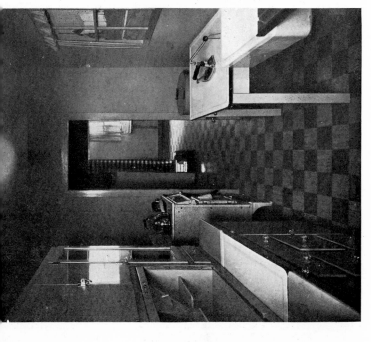

Fig. 127.—A Modern Kitchen.

[By courtesy of Building Centre, Ltd.

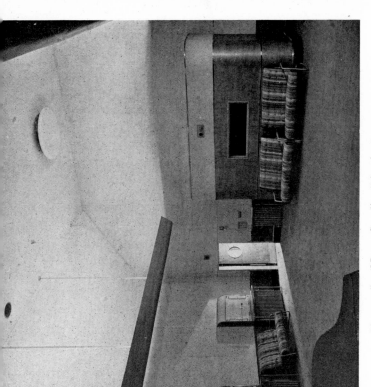

Fig. 126.—No. 4 Studio, Birmingham, B.B.C.
(Serge Chermayeff, Architect.)

FIG. 128.—Departmental Store, Schocken Chemnitz, Germany.
(Built 1930.)

(Erich Mendelsohn, Architect.)

FIG. 129.—The L.M.S. Hotel, Morecambe, 1933.

(Oliver Hill, Architect.)
[*By courtesy of London, Midland & Scottish Railway Compan*

organized a competition, and its results have been incorporated in an interesting booklet, " Industrial Housing in Wartime " (published by the R.I.B.A. at 1s. net). Various experiments were suggested, but in every case the windows are, for wartime, reduced to mere slits, for they constitute the chief danger, apart from a direct hit or near miss, through the admission of splinters and fragments ; in some cases small walls are added in front of the entrances. The most practical methods appear to be the building of single storey houses which can be converted into a normal two-storey semi-detached dwelling in peace time by enlarging the openings and adding the first floor stage above. Meanwhile there is a 4-in. roof of solid concrete tied to the walls with reinforcing rods to stop it being blown off bodily. Some architects place their beds in recesses, with some approach to the old Scottish practice. Anyhow, by careful scheming, adequate protection is provided against blast and splinters, which is all that can be done without burrowing deep underground.

It is curious that after being heartily abused for a generation or so, the basement has staged a definite " comeback," and if deep and substantial, is regarded as a decided asset. Folding boxed shutters also are fine for the black-out after being grumbled at as an obsolete nuisance.

It is too early yet to say what effect the second world war will have on the design and construction of houses, offices, flats (when these come to be built again) and on factories, but there is no doubt that the possibility of aerial bombing will have a definite influence on planning and construction. Meanwhile it is interesting to note that the layout and sites will probably be irregular and inconspicuous to some extent, merging the habitations in the natural features, such as hedges and trees, giving from the air the impression of a settlement which has grown up haphazardly for two or three centuries, and still further reducing conspicuousness by ingenious camouflage.

CHAPTER V

PRODUCTION (Old Methods)

W E now wish to deal with the methods adopted by man in producing the everyday things he requires for living, and we shall contrast the old and new.

We shall use the building trade for the first, because it is the one of which we know most, but the methods we describe would have been equally applicable to the engineering trade. In the first of our periods the fitter, turner and pattern-maker were still handicraftsmen. Here and there the antique methods may survive, but " rationalization," which means substituting the machine for man, is at work and things become more mechanical each day—but this is how building and most other work was done in 1889. It so happened that in this year it was determined that one of the authors should pass twelve months in working in a builder's yard, and a very pleasant time it was, and the world went very well then. Looking back, the days are remembered as being full of interest, because the work itself was so interesting, and the men were full of character because they were doing men's work, and, though they did not know it, or talk about it if they did, they were all inheritors of a great building tradition and working in ways which had been handed down through thousands of years. Of course there was no nonsense talked about arts and crafts ; the only compliment one workman would pay to another was to say that he was a good tradesman.

These were the trades. First the navvy got to work and dug the trenches and mixed the concrete for the foundations, and as he did it all by hand he had to be a burly man. Followed the bricklayer and his labourer ; and here is a

138

point to be remembered—the tradesmen, like the brick-layers, carpenters and joiners, were the aristocrats, and the labourers were the labourers. The tradesmen would be kind and nice to the labourers—the latter were of the building fraternity, but most certainly were not admitted to equality. If there were any stone dressings to the brick-work the mason was called in, and had to have his work ready in time for the brickwork. By the time the first floor was reached the carpenter was called in to fix the wooden joists; no floorboards were fixed as yet, and one soon became quite used to running across these joists.

By this time the outside scaffolding had been fixed. This was done by a scaffolder, who ranked as a slightly superior labourer. It might be that some new poles were needed, and these were delivered, with their bark on, and it was a very pleasant job to strip this off with a draw-knife. Its resinous smell brought the countryside and the woodlands on to the job. That is another point of our memories: you never bought anything you could make; nowadays you never make anything you can buy.

So the work went on, and as the building rose the work of the labourers increased. All the bricks—twelve at a time—and mortar were carried up the ladders in hods on the labourers' shoulders. The labourers made the mortar. The sand was set out in a circular embankment and the lime put inside it, and then the water was added; the lime popped and burst, and sufficient heat was generated to warm the labourers' tea-can. Then it was all knocked up and mixed together. There was no mortar mill or anything of that sort—everything was done by hand.

The carpenter framed the roof and boarded it, and fixed the battens on which the slates or tiles were fixed, and then the slater or tiler got to work, and the plumber had to be at hand to fix any lead flashings or gutters. Now for the first time the builder had a roof over his head and was free from having the work stopped by weather. Of course no windows had been fixed, and the wind could blow through the building and dry it off a little—if it happened to be a north-easter it was cold indeed !

The plasterer had already looked ahead and made his lime and hair for plastering the walls and ceilings—this lime and hair was made very much like the mortar, only hair was added to bind it together. The hair arrived in tangled lumps to which lime dust had already been added. It was rather an unpleasant job for a labourer to tease the hair into a fluff by beating it with laths. He sat down at a board to do his work, and tied a handkerchief across his face just under the eyes.

Then there were the laths. These were not bought ready made and sawn, but rent out by a lath render, who did this work. The rent laths were very much better than the sawn ones, because the rending followed the grain and the slight waveyness meant that there was a better key for the plastering.

By this time the floors were being laid in the building. The plasterers needed a floor to work on, and, had they plastered the ceilings first, the hammering down of the floorboards over would have broken the key of the plastered ceilings under.

It was at the stage of floor-laying that one of the authors made his first acquaintance with the building trade. The floorboards were nearly an inch thick, and had to be laid down at right-angles to the floor joists and nailed to these with floor brads $2\frac{1}{2}$ inches long. Cramps were used to screw back the floorboards so that the joints between them were as close as possible, and then the fun began. One was provided with a pair of knee pads, made of thick carpet and tied on with tapes, a hammer with a claw on the other end to pull out badly-driven nails, and a handful of floor brads in the pocket of your carpenter's apron. You started work on hands and knees and crawled forward, always inclining the point of the nail a little towards yourself, so that when it was driven it tended to tighten up the joints between the boards. No bradawl was used to punch the holes; the expert made the nail stand up by itself with the first tap of the hammer, and then drove it home with two extra blows given with the full force of strong arms. The nails were then punched in and any irregularities between the thickness of the boards at the joints cleaned off with a smoothing plane.

The memory of that first day on a building will always linger. Toiling alongside Jim, of whom we shall have more to say, thumb joints were hit instead of the nails, or both were missed and the floorboards bruised instead, and at the end of the day one suffered from an imitation of " housemaid's knee " that was so good it might have been the real thing. Yet it was not a bad day though a very cold one. Jim, who was a mighty worker, actually steamed as he advanced across the floor to the accompaniment of a rhythm of blows which was never interrupted by a break through faulty driving of a nail. Then in the middle of the winter's afternoon, when every muscle was aching, arrived the boy with tea—there were always boys on the building, and one of them made the tea. His method was to buy the cheapest black tea and give it a good boil, and then add milk and sugar. It was served up in a tin beer can, nearly a quart of it, and you did not need a spoon. We do not know how the nectar of the gods was prepared, but it could not have been better than the tea drunk in that building on a winter's afternoon, when the sun was going down and frost began to make itself felt in the air.

Now Jim was the foreman carpenter and joiner. He came on to the building to fix his joists, frame his roofs and lay his floors, but his real home was the carpenter's shop in the builder's yard. Looking back, he is remembered as a thoroughly nice man, and of course a " good tradesman "; he had served his time and had been apprenticed to a country builder for seven years, and during that time had learned all that a good carpenter should know, and much more besides. He was of course a fine judge of timber. What gave Jim his fierceness was that he had tried his hand at building some houses on his own, and his business had not prospered and a lawyer had foreclosed, and Jim thought he had not been treated fairly ; he had been reduced to the ranks, and felt sore about it, so when he laid floors he drove his nails to a gentle accompaniment of swear words—every blow of his hammer killed a lawyer. It was almost as if he said, " There, take that "—bang. " Here is another for you "—wallop. Still he was no gloomy despot of the workshop we will now describe. It was a plain oblong brick building with plenty of windows, and a large pair of doors at one end, opening on to the yard, and a smaller one at the other end, opening on to the street, and through which timber was delivered. The roof was covered with pantiles, hung directly on to battens on the rafters, without any ceiling under, so the shop was hot in the summer, which did not very much matter because the large doors were always open ; but in the winter it could be very chilly, unless one emulated Jim's fury of working so that you steamed. In front of the double doors stood the grindstone and a mortice machine—this was the machinery section. The mortice machine was of the simplest type, where a chisel was moved up and down in a slide by a long handle. As you had to adjust the blade each time you reversed it, it was not used, because it was simpler to do the work by hand. Still the mortice machine stood there as a symbol of progress and made us all feel very up to date. As to the grindstone, turning this while Jim got the rounding out of one of his jack-plane irons was extremely hard work. Looking back, that is another point that is remembered, the superb condition in which the men kept their tools. The chisels had edges like razors, and, finished on an oil-stone, always had a final stropping on the palm of the hand before the edge was inspected. The teeth of the saws were sharpened by a file and then given the required set by a hammer—one tooth one way and the next the other, so that the saw cleared the sawdust out of the cut.

Saws bring one to the first job which was undertaken in

the shop, and this was to put a cut down the middle of a 9-inch by 2-inch deal so as to turn it into two door styles, as Fig. 130. The deal was laid flat on two carpenter's stools, and after having drawn a pencil line down the middle, one got to work with a rip saw (having larger teeth than those to a cross-cut saw), some linseed oil in a pot for a lubricant, and—ignominious mark of the beginner—a small square to test your saw and see if the cut was being made at right-angles to the face. You did not cut up the deal, which was a very good one (because in those days the timber was much better than it is now), without seeing that it was not wasted. Jim saw to all this—anyhow, a day's rip sawing was not much easier than a day's floor laying. You had to let the saw travel its whole length, and the expert drove it through the wood with never a buckle, and you never left your saw in the cut.

Having sawn out the styles and rails for your door, the next step was to plane them down to the required widths and thicknesses. Then followed the ploughing out of the grooves to take the panels, and the mortising and tenoning. Then the tenons were cut with a cross-cut saw back to the shoulder line, and the tenon cheeks, which left the tenon free to enter the mortice, with a fine tenon saw. In good work the panels were made of a lovely yellow pine, which has now gone out of use, and which was free from knots and did not split. If the panels were wider than the pine, two boards were joined by a rubbed glue joint, and if this was well done the panel would split before the joint gave.

In our shop Jim liked to leave all his joinery at this stage, so that the air might be free to get into the plough grooves and round the newly cut tenons and help to still further season the wood, and then there came a grand glueing-up day. The windows, stairs, dressers and cup-boards were all made in the same way by hand. Now all this work is done by the machine, and all that the un-fortunate joiner has to do is assemble the various parts and glue them up. No wonder he sometimes gets bored.

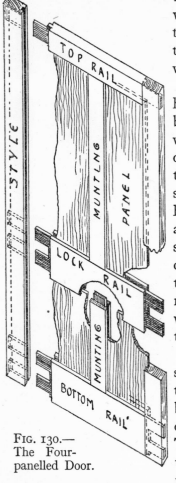

FIG. 130.—
The Four-
panelled Door.

If Jim could come back he would say, "Call 'emselves tradesmen, do they! Well, they are only doing labourers' work."

By this time the plasterer had finished his work on the building, and if the plastering was considered to have dried off sufficiently all of us went there, to do what was called the second fixing. This meant hanging the doors and fixing architraves and skirtings, and so on, and generally finishing off. A bench was taken on to the job, and mitre boxes and more tools, and generally the work called for more finish than the earlier carpentering.

So we might go on, but space precludes ; still we hope the little we have written will be sufficient to give some idea of how work was done in 1889. The point to be remembered is this : the old production methods kept many men usefully employed, and a man at work has money to spend, and so keeps other men employed ; the machine is a poor spender.

The pantiled workshop may sound very primitive, but if its equipment were poor the human element was very good indeed. Jim and his mates were clever and ingenious men, and full of character.

Here is a final tale of Jim. In his scanty leisure he bred black Spanish fowls and, wishing to sell a pair of these, he determined to advertise the fact in the local paper. What more natural to Jim than to write the advertisement out on a tenon cheek. Arrived at the office, an underling received the tenon cheek with scorn and called out to his mate, " Bill, I said somebody would bring in an advertisement written on wood, and here it is "—but they reckoned without Jim. The tale became one of the classics of the workshop, and we were always given to understand that, in the wordy battle that ensued it was the "clurk" who came off second best.

PRODUCTION (New Methods)

Production is based on power, and ever since the beginning of things man has sought to multiply his efforts by mechanical means. He must have used the lever to build Stonehenge. In our period he has made notable discoveries. In 1851 he was still dependent on Watt's steam engine, but by 1876 was beginning to experiment with the water turbine. Since then he has perfected it, and to-day, at the turbo-electric power plant at Niagara, the water is conducted to large penstock pipes, down which it descends with great force to be discharged against the blades of the turbine, which turns the shaft of the rotor generator, which produces the electricity. It is the old water-wheel come to life again.

Electricity has this great advantage—it can be used in a factory for one machine, or the whole plant (p. 149), or it can be transmitted over wide areas. It is no longer necessary to go where the power is—the power can be brought to you, and this fact may effect great alterations in industry. The individual craftsman may be helped by it.

This is the idea behind the post-war development of the transmission of electric power by the grid. As yet the cables which one sees looping across the country on their pylons are only used for high-voltage transmission to centres, but it is hoped that in the future this form of power will be more easily tapped.

In considering new methods, it will only be fair to leave

the Old World behind us and sail, or rather steam, across the Atlantic to America and, having landed in New York, take train to Detroit, the home of mass production. It will help us very much if on the journey we read " My Life and Work," by Henry Ford, because he, more than any other man, was the father of mass production, and at the same time one of the makers of the modern world. One of the authors was sent in 1928 to America, to inspect factories there and report on various aspects of factory planning, so the descriptions given, are of things seen.

Henry Ford, born at Dearborn, near Detroit, in 1863, was the son of a farmer, and his early life was like that of many other engineers. When he was twelve years old he was fired by the sight of a steam road engine ; at thirteen he could take a watch to pieces and put it together so that it kept time. At seventeen he was apprenticed to a machine shop, and while there heard of the Otto stationary gas engine. Ford repaired one in 1885, and then started building an experimental four-cycle gas engine himself—that is, one which works by induction, compression, explosion and exhaustion.

By this time the farmer father was seriously concerned with the son's liking for machinery, so 60 acres of timber-land were presented to him, a cottage was built, and Ford married—but there was a workshop at the back of the cottage, and experiments were carried on in it. By 1890 Ford had started on a two-cylinder engine, and then went back to engineering in Detroit at $45 a month. The house there had another workshop built in the back garden, and in it Ford worked in the evenings and holidays on his motor. Ford senior's plans came to nought, because Ford junior had married a Ford enthusiast—" But it was a very great thing to have my wife even more confident than I was. She has always been that way." This being the case, Ford produced in 1893 " the first, and for a long time the only, automobile in Detroit." The first Benz car reached New York in 1895, where Ford paid a visit to see it. The first

RACING

Ford proved a great nuisance in Detroit. The horses all bolted, but the people gathered in bunches to see the car pass, and if Ford stopped he was at once surrounded by a crowd.

The usual thing happened—a company was formed to exploit (disgusting word) the new car, with Ford as the chief engineer. From now on his history might have been that of any successful man who was out to make money at the expense of the public. But this was not Ford's idea at all ; it was not business as usual, but very unusual business, that he had in mind ; so he left the company in 1902—a fairly heroic proceeding for a young married man.

We were early motorists and can well remember the treatment we used to receive. The makers were affable and pleasant until they had got your money—and that was just the utmost they could screw out of you—and then all they wanted to see of you was your back. When the car broke down—which it invariably did—you were received with disfavour at the works, kept waiting for hours, and charged fabulous prices for spares. This was supposed to be good business.

Ford changed all this. After leaving the company he carried on his experiments. He did some racing, and there are amusing accounts in his book of a car he built for this purpose, with four cylinders, giving 80 h.p., and *tiller steering*. " Going over Niagara Falls would have been but a pastime after a ride in it," was the verdict, and one driver remarked on starting, " Well, this chariot may kill me, but they will says afterwards that I was going like hell when she took me over the bank "—but the chariot came through safely and finished half a mile ahead of all the others. This was useful advertisement.

Ford was now ready to found his own Ford Motor Company in 1903, but his own shareholders were not entirely tractable, so by 1906 he managed to obtain 58½ per cent. of the shares, which gave him control, and in 1919 his son, Edsel, bought the remainder, and had to pay $12,500 for every $100 share. Which looks as if the unusual business had proved to be better than business as usual.

MASS

When Ford was in control he put into practice his revolutionary ideas, and he was revolutionary at heart. A
fellow who waves a red flag and gets " run in " by the
police may be called a revolutionist, while in reality he is
just a nuisance. Ford, on the other hand, is a real revolutionist, because he has altered not only the production
of things, but the outlook of the business man all over the
world, and the end of the tale has still to be told.

He began by saying that " When one of my cars breaks
down I know I am to blame." Now the other motor manufacturers did not know this, or if they did they kept it to
themselves. Still they had to follow suit and the much
abused word " service " came into use. But Ford was the
man who made the car reliable ; hence the saying that
" You can dissect a Ford, but you cannot kill it."

His next idea was that he would sell his cars as cheaply
as possible. This of course was a monstrous proceeding
from the point of the ordinary business man. The car was
a novelty, people were just awakening to its possibilities ;
therefore " sting " them for it and keep up the price. Ford
argued that the motor was not a luxury but a necessity, and
that he was out to make motors for the million. The price
of his tourer was $950 in 1909, and had been reduced to
$360 in 1916. By May, 1921, Ford had made five million
cars. So all Ford's energies went in cutting prices, and in
doing this he discovered mass production. Every part of
the car was studied and simplified. Every operation in the
manufacture was very carefully considered, and nothing
which was hard or laborious was allowed to be done by
hand if it could be done instead by a machine. The workman must not exhaust himself by having to lift heavy
weights. An idea was gained from the Chicago meat
packers. When a man is dressing a heavy carcass of beef
he does not carry it around on his shoulders, but suspends
it from an overhead trolly, so that it can be readily moved.
In this way the first moving assembly line was being experimented with in April, 1913, and the moving line (see

FIG. 132.—Boots' Factory, Nottingham.
(Sir Owen Williams, Architect.)
[By courtesy of " The Architect and Building News."

FIG. 131.—Interior of Laboratory of Henry Ford at Dearborn, Detroit, U.S.A.
[By courtesy of Albert Kahn, architect of the building.

FIG. 123.—The Main Assembly Line at the Cowley Factory, near Oxford.

Figs. 133–136) is the essence of mass production, because, instead of the workman having to walk about the workshop, the work comes to him, and while it passes he does the one job which is his particular work. The customer as well had to be disciplined; for example, he could have any colour he liked so long as it was black.

It was in January, 1914, when the moving assembly lines had been in use for some months, that Ford announced that the minimum wage, under certain conditions, for any class of work in his factories was to be $5, or £1, for an eight-hour day, and this was increased to $6 later. This created consternation all over the world among the employers—but why? Here was a man who by the use of mass production could produce a very good car at a very low price, pay very high wages, and yet make money in so doing. Ford had pointed the way to plenty, and it only remained for the other employers to follow suit and produce masses of things by mass production and sell them very cheaply, and hunger and cold need be feared no longer. But this they could not do, and did not realize that in April, 1913, and January, 1914, a new order of production had come into being which could not be denied.

By the kindness of Mr. Albert Kahn the architect, of Detroit, we are enabled to publish a view of the inside of the laboratory which he designed for Mr. Ford (Fig. 131). This is an experimental workshop, in which all new ideas are tried out. We saw it when we were at Dearborn in 1928, and it is the finest industrial interior we have ever seen. The construction is in concrete and steel, and all the upper part is painted. The whole of the floor is covered with polished maple. On this the machinery is set out in an orderly fashion. In front of each machine is a rubber mat, and a neat cabinet for the tools. The machinery is driven by motors, and there are no unsightly pulleys and shafting. All cables are in a basement. We remember in one of the bays a large printing press with plenty of space around it, so that it could be seen, and kept all glittering and bright like the inside of a watch. It was really a beautiful sight. All the lavatories were in the basement, and these would not have disgraced a West-End club in London. That is one very good point about American factories—the sanitary accommodation is always excellent. That filthy thing the round towel is never used. An American employer once tried to introduce it, but he was taken outside and hanged from a tree with it, which discouraged others from following suit. Generally a paper towel is used, and then thrown into a basket. In some places you press a knob and dry your hands over a hot-air blast.

When we were at Dearborn, going over the Ford plant, we could not help thinking of it in comparison with the little workshop which we have described, and in which we worked ourselves in 1889. Like Jim and his friends, that has passed on, except perhaps in the villages, and though we may regret it for many things, it cannot be restored. It produced good things, but not plenty; quality but not quantity. If, however, we accept mass production in its stead, we must accept as well certain other conditions that go with it. Mass production means low prices, high wages, short hours and leisure for all. Some early and mid-century industrialists—quite honestly, one hopes— believed in low wages, long hours and high prices, and to attain these were willing to employ infants in mines, and all the forces of law and order were on their side. The whole pitiful tale can be read in Mr. and Mrs. Hammond's books on the Village Labourer and the Town Labourer.

Then prices must be kept up. Even in the first Great War, when men were being killed for want of shells, the armament manufacturers fought hard to keep up prices, not so much because they were inhuman, but rather as a sacred duty laid on them. This is one of the terrible things, that it is still possible to make profit out of war. There is nothing disturbs these people so much as plenty, and they call it a glut to show their disapproval. You read that there is a glut of herrings, or wheat, or some other com-

FIG. 134 (with Figs. 135 and 136).—The

(From a drawing specially made b

t the Cowley Works of Morris Motors, Ltd.

(1 artist of " The Motor "—*Copyright*.)

FIG. 135 (with Figs. 134 and 136).—The
(From a drawing specially made by

the Cowley Works of Morris Motors, Ltd.

FIG. 136 (with Figs. 134 and 135).—The

(From a drawing specially made by

the Cowley Works of Morris Motors, Ltd.

artist of " The Motor "—*Copyright.*)

modity, and, instead of thanking God on their knees for His bounty, the herrings are allowed to rot and the corn is burned, because if this were not done the prices of commodities would go down, and from their point of view that would be disastrous. Now this is very extraordinary, because, if the exchange of commodities is the basis of commerce, then plenty should be exchanged for plenty, to the benefit of all.

There is no doubt that an extension of the principles of mass production could produce shorter hours, higher wages and plenty for all. If the jobbers, brokers, dealers, distributors and speculators would only realize : " Speculation in things already produced—that is not business ; it is just more or less respectable graft," all might be well. If not, we shall have to remind them that people in the Middle Ages who bought goods on the way to market, with the idea of raising prices, and others who attempted to corner goods were called " fforstallers " and " regrators," and they were put in the pillory—and the pillory is a useful institution which could very readily be mass produced once more.

Now we have a pleasant task, and that is to write of another William Morris, whose name is connected with Oxford. This William Morris (now Lord Nuffield), after he had been apprenticed to a cycle maker for a few months, determined that, as he had learned all his principal could teach him, he would set up in business on his own account. He had reached the mature age of seventeen, and his capital was a few pounds he had saved from his pocket money, but he built good bicycles and sold them at a low price, and the business prospered. Then Morris turned his attention to cars, and we remember how a friend of ours, in 1912, bought one, and a very good car it was. Then the 1914 War came on and Morris made munitions, and munition-making taught manufacturers a good deal about quantity production.

After the first World War he started up on car-making again, and all English boys and girls know of the group of cars coming from the Morris factories. Figs. 134, 135 and 136, which have been kindly placed at our disposal by Morris Motors Ltd., illustrate in three sections a bird's-eye view of the great hall at the Cowley works, showing various types of chassis on their assembly lines, the overhead conveyors (called telphers), drying ovens, etc. Fig. 133 shows in detail part of these main assembly lines, which render possible the production of the cars at the price they are sold. It was at Cowley that mass production was first introduced into this country, and this made it possible to reduce the two-seater Cowley from £375 in 1921 to £165 in 1933, and allowed the car to be improved all the time. In 1939 their 8 h.p. two-seater sold for £132 10s. and their 10 h.p. saloon for £175. The public like the cuts in prices possible under these methods, but they long for something individual, so the manufacturers have had to give way in colour, and now offer quite a range.

Another interesting detail is that the modern factory system has called into being a whole new class of people. In the old workshop the master looked after the business side, with perhaps one clerk to help him, and the foreman, like Jim, was a working foreman. In the big factory there may be a doctor, who medically examines the workmen, and nurses to see to their injuries. Welfare superintendents look after the social side, and canteens feed them. The raw materials may be tested in laboratories, and the products during manufacture. The work is set out in drawing offices, and other men prepare the jigs for the automatic machines. There are all the clerks, who attend to the clerical work, and a high-powered sales organization, which persuades the public that it must buy or die. In many factories producing, say, a cardboard carton, or a paper drinking cup, or a tin box, which nobody really wants, the factory itself is far more wonderful than its product.

There have been extraordinary developments in what may be called the packing industries. To take one example, only a few years ago, if you wanted to buy tobacco, you went to the tobacconist, who weighed you out, say, 2 ounces, which you put in your pouch. With this you filled your pipe or made cigarettes. It might be shag or navy cut, but it had no particular brand. Then it occurred to certain manufacturers that, if the tobacco were packed in tins, and the cigarettes in cartons, the public would pay more for something which they thought was better. This led to great developments in advertising, because each proprietary brand had to be advertised as being the very best, and the brands had to be packed in an endless variety of ways. All this adds to cost and is a charge borne by the customer. As well it adds to the litter problem, because all the packages are thrown away. It is commercialized waste, which was learnt to be rigorously salvaged in the 1939 war.

We have dealt with production thus fully because it is a subject of great importance—perhaps the greatest, because it deals with the way masses of men are to spend their lives. If it does lead, as it well may, to plenty, well and good ; but this must be established, or we shall have sold our freedom to do interesting work very dearly. Clearly it would have been very unsafe to have placed so much power in the hands of the early Victorian industrialists. The men who pleaded that they could not conduct their business to profit without the aid of pauper infants working in their mills would have ground us all to slavery by mass production, had it been invented then, because it needs no skill. There is no need for a seven-years' apprenticeship as happened to our friend Jim (p. 141)—seven hours will easily teach you your one little job. Nor need you be very intelligent. The natives in Africa already work in the mines, and could just as easily work on the moving assembly line. All this is felt, and already in America the net of control is being cast over the industrialist lest he bestride the world like a colossus.

DISTRIBUTION

This is a subject which is sure to engage the attention of our readers as they grow older, because it represents one of

Fig. 137.—Original Store of Rochdale Pioneers (now a
Co-operative Museum).

the greatest modern problems—How are we to distribute
the plenty which is made possible by mass production ?

In the Middle Ages the market place was the great
distributing agency, and around it were grouped such
shops as were necessary—the tailor, shoemaker, saddler
and so on. In Vol. II, p. 110, we gave Celia Fiennes
description of how the spinners, weavers, dyers and fullers
dealt with their serge in Exeter market. In Vol. III, p. 120,
we gave Cobbett's views on the utility of markets to small
craftsmen who, having made things, *could offer them in the
market directly to the purchaser.* Commodities were exchanged with little cost added for the exchange. There
were very few dealers, jobbers, brokers and commission
agents whose charges had to be added.

In the nineteenth century the "fforstaller" and "regra-
tor" began to be able to put on the guise of respectability,
because—as the population increased, and the goods made
in the factories were sent overseas and were paid for by
imported foodstuffs, business became less local and direct

and had to pass through many more channels—the dealer came into his own.

We see the beginnings in the Farington Diary. The painter was at Shipston-on-Stour in 1801, and talked to Roche, a civil and intelligent man, who kept the " George " there. Roche complained that a spirit of monopoly had arisen and, increasing daily, was being extended to almost every article of life. There were people who made it their business to go to the farmers and cottagers and purchase fowls, eggs, garden stuff, and so on. The growers were saved trouble, but the dealers, having the monopoly, put up prices so that the people at large suffered. There can be no doubt that poor people in the early nineteenth century did suffer. Their attempts to improve the conditions of life for themselves by co-operation form one of the romances of the century.

In 1769 certain poor Ayrshire weavers clubbed together to buy oatmeal, and, on a much bigger scale, 1435 poor townsmen of Hull combined, in 1797, to own a windmill and so protect themselves from " covetous and merciless men." Other societies were formed—there was the North-west of England Co-operative Co. of Liverpool, in 1830, but the movement did not become national and seems to have been confined to the manufacturing districts, where Industrialism was rampant.

Charles Howarth seems to have been the first to link the idea that members should buy their goods, pay cash and then divide the savings by way of a dividend with a set of rules, which have been used as a model all over the world. This must be remembered—that the idea of co-operation has spread and is still spreading. One of the latest is the Palestine Co-operative Wholesale Society. Fig. 137 shows the little shop in which the Rochdale Pioneers started their business in 1844 ; it is now a Co-operative museum. By 1860, 200 societies had followed this example, but they were not as yet wholesalers or manufacturers. However, on Good Friday, 1863, 200 delegates met together in a hall at Ancoats, Manchester, and, sustained by a high tea at 6*d.* a head (plates of ham 3*d.* extra), decided to found the North of England Co-operative Wholesale Agency and Depot Society Ltd. Now (1934) there are three wholesale societies and 1171 retail societies in England, having a membership of 6,760,432, and their sales come to £201,221,581 a year. This is, and has been, largely a working-class movement, and it is one of the wonders of the nineteenth century.

This co-operative movement was largely an escape from tyranny, and the tough old operatives of the North who worked it out may have builded better than they knew—there is hope for the future in the movement if it is extended. It is the solution of the distribution problem. A man can work in one of the wholesale societies and make clothes, furniture or boots, for example, and buy the produce of his own or his friend's labour in the retail society—he saves all the ordinary costs of distribution, which are returned to him in dividends—or a smallholder who is a member of a retail society can take his fowls and eggs there and exchange them for groceries, or any other things he may require. The Co-operative Society serves the same purpose as the old market place—the "fforstaller" is forestalled.

It is this which makes us think that the solution of the troublous time which we are suffering may be found eventually in a great extension of co-operation. The world which was run on competition and profit has nothing so fine to show as the movement run on co-operation and saving, and this latter has been done by working men and women by themselves for themselves without any subsidies or quotas or outside assistance.

Governments seem to have a grudge against co-operation, perhaps because they cannot make co-operators pay income tax—but why should they when all that is done is to effect savings by co-operation? This nearly breaks the heart of the income tax officials, who, had they lived in Greek times, would have taken from the corpse the obol placed in its mouth for journey money to the spirit world.

As to ordinary trading in the nineteenth century, the unfortunate shopkeeper was expected to give credit, and cash payments were the exception. The honest customer paid for the dishonest one. Many tradesmen, however, tempted their customers to take credit—undergraduates, for example, in the older universities—because in this way they were enslaved and, labouring under a burden of debt, could hardly check prices, quantity or quality. Many men started their lives, on coming down, handicapped in this way.

Other people followed the co-operators' example. Some postal employees, who were not too well paid, combined together in the winter of 1864–65 to buy half a chest of tea from a wholesale house. They then divided this up, and found that they had saved 9*d*. a lb. and obtained a better tea. The Post Office authorities lent them a store cupboard as a warehouse, and coffee, sugar and a few other things were bought and split up in this way. Then a room had to be hired, and in 1865 the Post Office Supply Association threw their organization open to the whole of the Civil Service, and in 1866 became registered under the name of the Civil Service Supply Association.

In 1871 officers of the Army and Navy combined for the same purpose, and so the Army and Navy Co-operative Society came into being with their fine stores in Victoria Street, Westminster. The Society, however, is only co-operative in that it was founded to supply goods at the lowest remunerative prices, and dividends on profits are paid to shareholders only.

The ordinary shopkeepers followed suit, and the departmental store of to-day is one result of the example of the societies we have been describing. Their difficulties are found in that they all have to compete against one another, and to do so spend vast sums advertising their wares—and the shouting is paid for by the customer.

BANKING

As we said at the beginning, in Victorian times we were learning to produce things ; to-day the problem is how to distribute them. If you take a small provincial town as an example, you will probably find that its ancient market has fallen into disuse, and its place has been taken by retail tradesmen. Each of these has to maintain cars, carts and boys on bicycles to deliver the goods. If the total cost of the distribution of these goods could be added up it would form a surprising total.

Another difficulty which has arisen is that the improvement in transport has added to the difficulties of the small trader. In the village we described on p. 51, if the boot-maker and tailor continued to make good boots and breeches, their customers continued to employ them. To-day the cheap railway and the motor-bus whirl them up to the town, and their money is lost to the village. Again, the motor delivery vans bring goods from a distance. Trading has become like a game of unmusical chairs ; somebody is always being left without means of support, and anybody's turn may come next.

BANKING AND CURRENCY

Before we close this section on distribution, or the exchange of commodities, a word must be said about the money which is used as a medium for the exchange. We have seen in our books that money has taken strange forms at different times. Golden bracelets with rings fastened on them were used in the Bronze Age, and flat iron currency bars in the Early Iron Age—both of more value than the greasy bits of paper we use to-day. Still it does not very much matter what form the currency takes, if it is not counterfeited, and with it you can obtain the goods you desire.

Herodotus claimed that the Lydians of Asia Minor were the first to use gold and silver coins, and the Greeks adopted this money habit. They turned their coins into superb works of art, and we illustrated some in Fig. 49,

"Everyday Things in Classical Greece." Gold was found in Lydia, so the Lydians melted it down into ingots, and stamped these to guarantee their weight and quality. A Greek trader would exchange his pottery for their corn, or accept gold, if with it he could buy corn elsewhere. The price was settled by how much the customer desired the goods. Had the Lydian made good pottery himself, he would have suggested perhaps that the Greek brought olive oil.

Though trading has become much more complicated than this, the exchange of commodities is its basis. This fact has been lost sight of. There are people who gamble in money. It is of course quite possible to buy money—you have to do so to go abroad. But if you buy francs cheap with the idea of making them scarce and sending up the price, or if you buy gold and hoard it, you are depriving the trader of his medium for the exchange of goods. These are unsocial acts, and the people who do these things should be bastinadoed and then banished.

Nevertheless, with all defects and shortcomings industry and trade abound in wonderful achievements, and produce goods in an infinite variety to satisfy everyone's needs, and send them to every quarter of the globe till war comes to interrupt their connections. Let us get away from the curious idea that there is anything intrinsically immoral or wrong about "making a profit"; the process needs to be kept within reasonable bounds or it becomes extortion, but there is no fundamental cleavage between "profit" and "service"—the two are indissolubly linked, and the ideal is service *and* profit—no service, no profit. The manufacturer and seller aim to please their public and serve them well, and have to do it to succeed. The profits of industry and trade supply the nation's revenue by the taxes levied on them; if this source were to fail or be cut off, the wheels would stop turning.

CHAPTER VI

THE PUBLIC HEALTH

NOW we come to what is the most important chapter in this book. The public health is a matter of the greatest moment to the community, and until quite recently good health was rather a lottery. There were cholera epidemics in London in 1848–49, and again in 1853–54. There were 18,036 deaths in the first, and nearly 20,000 in the second. That the public health was improved was very much the work of one man, Pasteur. Sir William Osler, the Regius Professor of Medicine at Oxford, writing of him, said : " At the middle of the last century (1850) we did not know much more of the actual causes of the great scourges of the race, the plagues, the fevers and the pestilences, than the Greeks. Here comes in Pasteur's great work. Before him Egyptian darkness ; with his advent a light that brightens more and more as the years give us ever fuller knowledge."

Pasteur (born 1822) was the son of a tanner, who married a gardener's daughter with the pleasant name of Jeanne Etiennette Roqui. The father was a man of parts, who had fought in the Napoleonic Wars as a sergeant-major, and on discharge was decorated with the ribbon of the Legion of Honour. Like most French families, the Pasteurs were devoted to one another, and one touching thing about Louis was that he was never to become greater in his own estimation than his tanner father ; always he kept him in touch with his experiments and explained them so that they could be understood.

We cannot follow his education here, but his first discovery was the crystal formation of tartaric acid. In

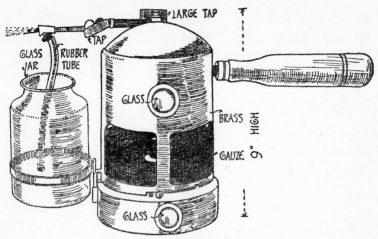

FIG. 138.—Lord Lister's Spray.
(*Royal College of Surgeons, London.*)

1849 he was appointed Professor of Physics at Strasburg University, and here it was that Pasteur met his future wife, who was one of the daughters of the Rector, rather above him in social standing. He fell in love, and so addressed a letter to his Rector, stating that his father was a tanner in the small town of Arbois, in the Jura, but that, as he was determined that his sisters should have his share, he was without fortune—" My only means are good health, some courage, and my position in the Université "—and that his father would come to Strasburg to make the proposal of marriage.

In 1854 Pasteur was made Professor and Dean of the new Faculté des Sciences at Lille, and here it was that he came in contact with a M. Bigo, who was in difficulty with the manufacture of beetroot alcohol. This was the starting point of his work in fermentation, which he presented in a paper to the Lille Scientific Society in August, 1857, destined to become famous. Pasteur discovered that fermentation was caused by minute living organisms, and from this was led to his deduction that putrid and suppurative diseases might also be caused by the " infinitely little." Before this people had thought that matter decomposed or rotted away ; Pasteur showed that it did not die, but was resolved by a form of life.

Our own Joseph Lister, then a young surgeon in Glasgow, put Pasteur's principles into practice. He contributed a paper to the *Lancet* in 1867, in which he acknowledged his indebtedness to Pasteur and stated it was not the oxygen or other gaseous constituents of the air which produced decomposition, " but minute particles suspended in it, which are the germs of various low forms of life." This led Lister to invent his blow lamp, or spray, as Fig. 138, which is now in the Museum of the Royal College of Surgeons, in Lincoln's Inn, London. This blew a solution of carbolic acid over the surgeon and patient during the operation and created an antiseptic atmosphere, and if the operation were a long one the surgeon was wet through at the end. The lamp was the means of saving innumerable lives, and it enabled the surgeon to extend the range of his operations. All the instruments, sponges and surgeon's hands were purified in this way, and the same care was taken with the dressings.

Before Lister the surgeons paid very little attention to cleanliness. The general practice was to keep an old coat for operating, and the more bloodstained the better—it looked like good business, but it was a very bad business for the patient, who was doomed the moment the surgeon came near him. Lister's methods were not at once adopted. A distinguished old surgeon once told us that when he was a student one of the professors referred to Lister's work in an amused sort of way, and finished by saying that he did think every surgeon should have a bath at least once a week. So the mortality continued—in 1868, in French hospitals, the mortality after amputation was 60 per cent, but with Lister thirty-four out of forty survived, so gradually his methods were adopted. Fig. 139 shows an operation in progress about 1880 with the Lister spray at work. The surgeons are still wearing their frock coats. White coats seem to have been introduced about 1885.

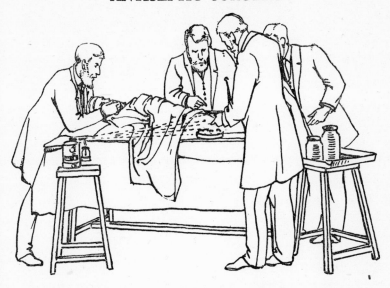

FIG. 139.—Operation of 1880 with Lister Spray in use. From " Antiseptic Surgery," by W. Watson Cheyne.

To return to Pasteur, from 1865–70 he was engaged in a campaign in finding the causes of a disease which was ruining the silkworm industry, and this he did. In 1871 he visited England in connection with brewing ; from 1873–77 he studied contagious diseases, and in the latter year began his great work against anthrax. It was not till 1881 that he announced the discovery of a vaccine against this terrible disease which had attacked the cattle of France. There followed a wonderful trial on sheep, which succeeded. By this time his critics were beginning to be silenced—the extraordinary thing is that Pasteur was not at once hailed as a genius.

In 1884 Pasteur began his work on hydrophobia. No one had been able to find a cure for this awful scourge, caused by the bite of a mad dog. By 1885 Pasteur had succeeded in rendering dogs immune, but dreaded making the experiment on man ; hitherto he had only worked on animals. Then a very dramatic thing happened—a little Alsatian boy of nine, who had been very badly bitten, was sent to Pasteur to be inoculated, and he was a very charming little fellow. Dare he do it ? The boy would certainly die, and that terribly, if he did not. Pasteur determined to take the risk, but, perhaps because of the age of the patient, he found the suspense very terrible. However, the inoculation was successful, and the boy was cured and lived happily ever after.

The whole world was moved. Here was a man—a great man indeed—who could cure hydrophobia, but he had done so in his spare time, at his own expense, and without any fee or reward. Pasteur, in fact, was very poor. When the good news was spread abroad patients began to find their way to Paris from all over the world ; a child of five was sent from New York ; some peasants from Russia. So subscriptions were raised—again from all over the world— and 2,586,680 francs were subscribed and the Pasteur Institute founded. The English Government appointed a commission in 1886, which reported that it would be difficult to over-estimate the utility of the discovery.

On Pasteur's seventieth birthday, in 1892, all the nations sent deputations to Paris to aid the celebrations. The Royal Societies of London and Edinburgh's deputy was our own Lord Lister, who said in his speech, " You have raised the veil which for centuries had covered infectious diseases ; you have discovered and demonstrated their microbian nature " ; and when Lister had concluded his address Pasteur walked across and embraced him. A distinguished English surgeon who was there told us that it was an extraordinarily moving sight to see these two great men together who had done so much for suffering humanity. Disraeli once said that a great nation is a nation which produces great men, and here were two truly great men, united in friendship, in a great common cause, and actuated by absolutely unselfish motives.

Pasteur described himself as " a man whose invincible belief is that Science and Peace will triumph over Ignorance and War, that nations will unite, not to destroy, but to

FIG. 140.—Present-day Surgical Operation.

build, and that the future will belong to those who will have done most for suffering humanity." Such a belief is an explanation of the work he did. Koch, the German chemist, did good work on Pasteur's lines—how splendid it would be if Frenchman, German and Englishman could unite to build instead of arming against one another to destroy! Our own Huxley said, " Pasteur's discoveries alone would suffice to cover the war indemnity of five milliards paid by France to Germany in 1870 "—and he was a kindly man. Here is a quotation from an address given by Pasteur to students at Edinburgh in 1884 : " The common soul (if I may so speak) of an assembly of young men is wholly formed of the most generous feelings, being yet illumined with the divine spark which is in every man as he enters this world."

We should like to think that all boys and girls would read Vallery-Radot's " Life of Pasteur." It is a great book about a great man, and the reading could well be

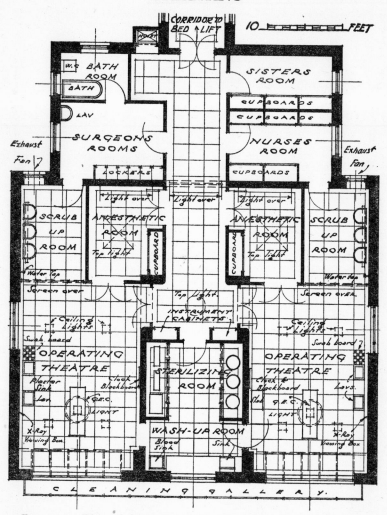

FIG. 141.—Plan of Operating Suite, Worcester Royal Infirmary.
(*Adams, Holden and Pearson, Architects.*)

taken as a test. If it moves you, then the road is clear and you can go forward. But if you are bored with this man who served Science, then obviously the spark has gone out or died down, and some form of spiritual bellows must be employed to see if it can be fanned into flame.

If our readers will refer back to Fig. 139 they will notice that, with the exception of the Lister spray, very few precautions of an antiseptic nature appear to have been taken. Very frequently the patient was wheeled into the operating room and placed under the anæsthetic there, which in itself was a considerable shock. In Fig. 141, kindly provided by Messrs. Adams, Holden and Pearson, is shown a modern operating theatre block. The patient is put under the anæsthetic in a separate room, and the most elaborate precautions are taken in sterilizing, so that the surgeons work under conditions of the most absolute cleanliness. Some credit for this must be given to the architects.

The discovery of X-rays by Röntgen in 1895, and of radium by the Curies, are other notable happenings. With these the surgeon can find out what is the matter with his patient before he operates. Sun-bathing, light cures and much healthier dress are all helping, so year by year the light brightens and the public health is improved.

SANITATION

In Vol. III we dealt fairly fully with internal sanitary fittings, so that we need do no more here than remind our readers that it was as late as 1871 that the Prince of Wales (later King Edward VII) caught typhoid fever while staying at a house in Yorkshire, and this was traced to bad drainage. This state of affairs inside the house was remedied by a group of men which included Chadwick, Corfield, Field, and S. Stevens Hellyer, and the latter embodied the principles of modern sanitation in a series of lectures given at the Society of Arts in 1881. But while improvements were being effected inside the house, grave complications arose outside. The water-closet at first was not a water-closet at all. Even in London it consisted of a shed in the garden with a seat in it, the sewage being discharged into a cesspool under. This when the town was a small place was not so terrible as it sounds, and the sewage filtered itself away into the gravel on which London is built. It is marvellous how the good earth cleanses itself. Then water-closets, flushed with 2 or 3 gallons of water, were invented and put into the houses and connected up to the cesspools with pipes. Then baths began to be more general, and the water from these went to the cesspools too, and these speedily became inadequate, so permission had to be given to connect up to the sewers. Up till 1815 this had not been permitted; then it was allowed, and by 1847 made compulsory.

These sewers were not part of a complete system as they are to-day. If reference is made to Sir George Humphreys' " Main Drainage of London " a very interesting map will be found of the Site of London, showing the ancient water-courses. Starting from the east, on the north side of the Thames, there was the Black Ditch and Shoreditch; then the Wall Brook and the Fleet, the King's Scholars' Pond (Tyburn), Ranelagh, and Stamford Brook. In course of time these streams were covered in and became sewers for storm water, and it was into these that sewage was discharged. The Metropolitan Commission of Sewers came into being in 1847, and 200,000 cesspools were done away with, but the immediate effect of this was that the Thames itself became a vast sewer, because all the streams, which had been turned into sewers, discharged into the river.

This may have been partly responsible for the cholera epidemics of 1848–49 and 1853–54, when 38,036 people died in London. In 1855 the Metropolitan Board of Works was formed to try and improve matters. One great difficulty was that the Thames is a tidal river. At high tide the sewage was held up in the sewers, and at low tide foul mud was exposed. Complaints were made in the House of Commons in 1858 that " it was a notorious fact that hon. gentlemen sitting in the committee rooms and the library were utterly unable to remain there in consequence of the stench which arose from the river." Small wonder that the Thames became deserted. In the seventeenth century Pepys tells us how he went " to the Cherry Garden and then by water singing finely to the Bridge, and there landed." The nineteenth-century Londoner could not do this. Though devoid of taste, he yet possessed the sense of smell.

This raises a rather interesting point. Certain enthusiasts point to the Middle Ages, and sing of the cathedrals and colourful life then. " Ah," say their opponents, " remember the dirt." All we can say is that the mediæval people would have had to be very grubby to have been grubbier in their habits than the nineteenth-century folk.

The Board of Works, when they got to work, constructed intercepting sewers, which cut across the lines of the old ones and conveyed the sewage well to the east of London, at Barking on the north side, and Crossness on the south, where, after treatment, it was discharged on the ebb tide—but all this took a very long time to do. The Commissioner of Sewers had invited plans and suggestions in 1849 ; Joseph Bazalgette prepared designs in 1853, and when the Board of Works came into being in 1855 they said something must be done " on or *before* the 31st of December, 1860." Sir Joseph Bazalgette, who was now Chief Engineer to the Board of Works, did finally carry out the work, and handsomely acknowledged the help he had received from earlier schemes. The northern outfall works were completed in 1864, and the southern was opened by the Prince of Wales (Edward VII) in 1865. So it is only eighty years since London became habitable with any measure of safety, and the work of making this possible lasted from 1847 to 1864.

The good work was carried on. In 1876 the Rivers Pollution Prevention Act was passed, which forbade the discharge of untreated sewage into streams. The Act covers discharge into an estuary and the sea. There is a saving clause that discharge into the sea is not an offence if allowed after Government inquiry, and many seaside towns do this, and it is not a very pleasant idea. Why poison the fishes ?

The treatment of sewage to render it harmless can be traced back to Pasteur. He discovered that certain organisms, called anaerobic, work without oxygen, and will, if the sewage is passed through a closed tank, break down the solids in it. There are other organisms, called aerobic,

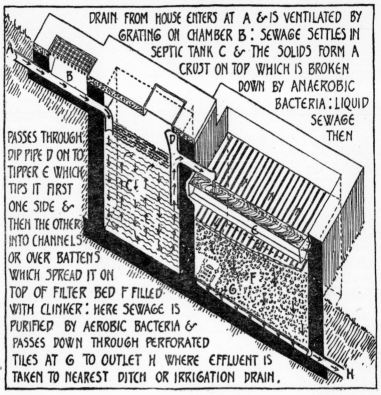

DRAIN FROM HOUSE ENTERS AT A & IS VENTILATED BY GRATING ON CHAMBER B : SEWAGE SETTLES IN SEPTIC TANK C & THE SOLIDS FORM A CRUST ON TOP WHICH IS BROKEN DOWN BY ANAEROBIC BACTERIA : LIQUID SEWAGE THEN PASSES THROUGH DIP PIPE D ON TO TIPPER E WHICH TIPS IT FIRST ONE SIDE & THEN THE OTHER INTO CHANNELS OR OVER BATTENS WHICH SPREAD IT ON TOP OF FILTER BED F FILLED WITH CLINKER : HERE SEWAGE IS PURIFIED BY AEROBIC BACTERIA & PASSES DOWN THROUGH PERFORATED TILES AT G TO OUTLET H WHERE EFFLUENT IS TAKEN TO NEAREST DITCH OR IRRIGATION DRAIN.

FIG. 142.—Half-sectional Isometric View of Sewage Disposal Plant for Small House.

which work in the open air, so if the broken-down sewage is passed through trickling filters the final process of purification can be accomplished. Fig. 142 explains the system. This is just one more thing Pasteur did, wherefore we say that he was a very great man; perhaps the very greatest who has ever lived. When the sword is finally beaten into the ploughshare he will be remembered, because the future belongs to those who will unite to build, not destroy. And the others, the dictator-destroyers, will all have descended into the dwelling of Hades and dread Persephone. There they will march and countermarch, and the worst that can happen then will be that sometimes the beat of their muffled drums will escape into the upper air.

CHAPTER VII

TRANSPORT AND COMMUNICATIONS

IN the Middle Ages men lived confined within the walls of their cities, and the stranger who passed through their gates was warmly welcomed if he could tell them of the world outside ; they were hungry for news. Froissart's Chronicles are the tales he told to his friends.

Then in the fifteenth century the Turks captured Constantinople, and the scholars there fled to Italy ; Columbus discovered America, and Caxton started printing, so that all these wonders could be made known far more widely than had been possible in the Middle Ages. The whole character of the peoples, and the lives they led, and the appearance of the things they made, were changed, and the Renaissance came in.

If the discovery of printing was one of the contributing causes of this great change, what are we to say of the nineteenth-century discoveries : the cables and telephones, fast cars, turbine-driven steamers, and aeroplanes ; and the greatest wonder of all—broadcasting ? The latter so well named, because it does actually broadcast intelligence over the whole wide world. Remember the programmes of Christmas, 1932 and 1933, when greetings were relayed all round the Empire and the King spoke to all his peoples. Think of the possibilities of wireless. Used in the wisest way, in the right hands, it is the greatest instrument yet devised for the leading forward of men and women. With it a new England may be built. In the hands of bad men its power for evil would be appalling, and fools could spread their folly just as widely.

The point we wish to make is this : All these things are

going to make great changes in the lives of men, and just as school-children of to-day learn of Caxton and his press, so in a few hundred years their successors will be told of Marconi and his wireless as one of the makers of the modern world.

Fig. 143 shows the fat, comfortable world at the beginning of our period, when the horse was supreme on land, and people rode and drove in broughams and landaus ; when there were no aeroplanes in the sky, or wireless, or cars.

We will detail these wonders in the order in which they were invented. We noted in Vol. III how Faraday in England, and Henry in America, by their discovery of electro-magnetic induction, brought electricity into use. It was not long before this was applied to the sending of messages. Wheatstone, a professor of King's College, London, and Morse, the American, were pioneers in this direction. The first public telegraph in England was erected in 1844, and worked by a system in which the letters of the message were recorded by the swings of a needle. This was generally superseded by that of Morse, which recorded in dots and dashes.

So much for the land, but all the while people were hoping it would soon be possible to communicate with the Continent, or even America. It is difficult for us now to realize that not so long ago the only method of communicating with our American friends was to send a letter by one ship and wait for the reply by another. In 1840 Wheatstone brought a project before the House of Commons of a cable between Dover and Calais. In 1843 Morse wrote to the Secretary of the U.S.A., and, after detailing experiments that he had made with a telegraph in 1844 between Washington and Baltimore, went on to say that he was confident communication could be established across the Atlantic. In 1848 Morse did stretch a submarine cable under New York harbour which recorded satisfactorily.

It can hardly be said that the enthusiasm was general, because when a Mr. Brett obtained a concession to lay a

FIG. 143.—Belgravia Out-of-Doors.
(" Bird's-eye Views of Society " Richard Doyle.)

cable across the Straits of Dover in 1850 the Press evidently regarded the idea as a gigantic swindle ; but the cable, of solid copper wire coated with gutta-percha, was laid and communication established for a little while.

After messages had come through for a few hours these failed. The explanation of this was that an industrious fisherman had pulled up the cable in his trawl and, having a good hack-saw on board, had cut out a section, which he took back to Boulogne and exhibited as a rare and precious sea-weed with a golden centre.

In 1851 another cable was laid across the Straits, of improved form, and this was successful. Others followed to Ireland and the Continent—but the Atlantic remained unconquered. Poseidon was still in command.

By 1857 the scientific men, who had been gaining experience by laying shorter cables, felt confident of success and turned their attention to the Atlantic once more. An American, Cyrus Field, was a moving spirit. A company was formed and the contracts let for making the cable. The great problem was how to lay it. It was quite simple to conceive the idea of making the cable and stowing it in the hold of a ship, and paying it out over the stern. But it was not so simple to be quite sure that the cable would sink to the bed of the ocean and rest there comfortably. There might be great submarine cliffs which would hold it suspended, or rocks among which it would writhe eel-like and chafe away its covering. Or Poseidon might send a great storm so that the cable might be snapped. All these things were very much in the mind of the men who were preparing to lay the cable. The English Government lent them the *Agamemnon* (Fig. 144), a new screw line of battle-ship, launched in 1852 ; and the U.S.A. the *Niagara*. One ship was to land the shore end of the cable at Valentia, on the west coast of Ireland, pay out her cable until it was exhausted ; the other was then to splice on her portion and carry on. A start was made on August 7th, 1857, but by the 11th, after laying 330 nautical miles, the cable broke

Fig. 144.—H.M.S. *Agamemnon* laying Atlantic Cable in 1858. A Whale crosses the Line. (From a contemporary drawing by Robert Dudley.)

in 2000 fathoms and the attempt was abandoned. The cable left was landed, and fifty-three miles of the shore end was recovered.

The attempt was renewed on June 10th, 1858. The same ships were employed, and decided to sail to mid-Atlantic, splice the cable there and then one go east, and the other west. The attempt failed by reason of fearful storms.

Ships again met in mid-Atlantic on July 28th, 1858, and this time they were successful. There were great rejoicings, and on August 18th the directors of the company in England sent this message : " Europe and America are united in telegraphic communication. ' Glory to God in the highest, on earth peace, good will towards men.' " This message took thirty-five minutes, and then on September 3rd no more messages came through and the cable failed. Something had happened, nobody knew what, but one solid fact was that half a million of money had been expended in vain.

By 1865 men had recovered their courage again and managed to raise some more money. The short success of the 1858 cable had shown the possibilities of telegraphic communication, so another start was made. This time it was decided to employ the *Great Eastern* (Fig. 145). This ship, designed by Brunel, the engineer to the Great Western Railway, was built between 1853–58 at a cost of £640,000. The ship was 692 feet long on the upper deck, 82 feet 6 inches broad, and 120 feet over the paddle-boxes, and the depth at side was 58 feet ; she was built of iron and driven by paddle and screw and, being much in advance of her time, had not proved at all profitable to her owners. Her dimensions were not exceeded until 1899. So this ship was chartered and Captain James Anderson, of the Cunard Co., put in command. A new cable of an improved type was made and stowed in three large circular tanks in the holds, and the *Great Eastern* could carry the whole cable.

The shore end was landed at Valentia in July, 1865, and then the *Great Eastern* put to sea and behaved splendidly ;

FIG. 145.—On Board the *Great Eastern*.   Searching for a fault after recovery of the Cable from the bed of
the Atlantic.
(From a contemporary drawing by Robert Dudley.)

nor were the cable layers worried by her ghost. The story went that while she was being built a plate riveter, who was lost somewhere in the internals of the ship, was himself riveted in, and after death his ghost moved about tap-tapping to be released. However that may be, the *Great Eastern* behaved splendidly at sea, but the cable-laying did not go on so well, as there were faults in the cable. These, however, were speedily repaired and, in Dr. Russell's words in the *Atlantic Telegraph*, " The communication with shore continued to improve, and was, in the language of tele-graphers, O.K.," which shows this expression not to be so modern after all—and then in 2500 fathoms an actual break occurred.

Now picture the anxiety not only on the ship, but in Europe. The *Great Eastern* was of course in communication with the shore at Valentia and could send messages over that part of the cable that was laid. Each time a fault was discovered the defect was remedied and a reassuring message sent home, so that the people there knew all that was happening on board ; then when the ship was two-thirds across the Atlantic—silence.

The wiseacres got to work and reminded everybody how they had foretold disaster. Undoubtedly the ship had gone down with all, or rather more than all, hands. There was no wireless to tell all the world of the frantic attempts which were being made on board, first to find the broken end, and then to grapple it and bring it to the surface ; no reporter to send out snappy copy of the three attempts which failed, not owing to lack of strength in the cable, but weakness in the hauling gear. So this attempt failed and Poseidon seemed destined to reign undisturbed over the Atlantic.

But another attempt was made in 1866, and not only was an entirely new cable laid, but the old one of 1865 was picked up and completed. A triumphant end to as courage-ous an endeavour as was ever made by man. Many were associated in it, and their names can be read in Dr. Russell's

FIG. 146.—Coasting Downhill on Boneshaker (1869) ; front
wheel 36 in. diameter.
(*Science Museum, London.*)

book—one outstanding name is that of Professor William
Thomson, who after became Lord Kelvin. Fig. 145 is
interesting because it shows that the " bridge " on the *Great
Eastern* was an actual bridge from a central deck-house
across to the two paddle-boxes. In the sailing ship the
officer in charge had to be at the stern of the ship so that
he could watch his sails, and the man at the wheel was near
him, and the ship did not sail straight ahead. The steamer
did, so the bridge came into being and, being higher up
and more mid-ship, gave a clearer view.

It was about 1868 that the boneshaker bicycle, as Fig.
146, was introduced into England from France. This was

the first really popular bicycle. The hobby horse (1818) and the Macmillan bicycle of 1839, which we illustrated in Vol. III, were not very practical, but with the boneshaker the young man could go out on high adventure. It was the equivalent of the motor-bike. The father of one of the authors did actually, about 1869, ride fifty miles down into Kent on a boneshaker. There was no gearing, and the wooden wheels had iron tyres.

The next date of consequence is 1869, when the Suez Canal was opened. This solved a problem which had long worried men. We saw in our book on Archaic Greece (p. 14) how Seti 1, in the fourteenth century B.C., cut a canal and joined the Nile and the Red Sea, and this was enlarged by Necho (612 B.C.). The final solution was the work of a Frenchman, Ferdinand de Lesseps. The immediate effect was to alter the whole system of communication with India, the Far East and Australia.

To go back a little. In the Middle Ages the Mediterranean was a busy trading centre, doing a considerable trade with India, goods being transhipped and taken overland on the line of the present canal. Then the sultans of Egypt began to be troublesome, so the sailors put their heads together to discover another route. One may have remembered the voyage round the Cape described by Herodotus, because Vasco de Gama rediscovered the Cape route in 1497. This being adopted, trade in the Mediterranean suffered. The same thing happened in 1869 ; trade flowed back to the Mediterranean and the Cape did not see so many tall ships.

A Tramways Act was passed in 1870. People were moving out of the centre of London into the suburbs, so traffic was increasing. The first trams ran on lines and were horse drawn.

It was in 1876 that Bell discovered that the vibration in the air set up by the voice could be caught up by a thin sheet of iron and transmitted by wires to a receiver. So the telephone system came into being. With the cables

FIG. 147.—The " Coventry " Tricycle for Sedate Riders (1876).
(*Science Museum, London.*)

all that happened was that you agitated a needle or received
dots and dashes, but now you could hear the actual voice.
Still the telephone did not at once become popular. We
remember installing one about 1897, in our ardent youth,
and being warned of its danger. A client might ring you
up and give you instructions, and then go back on them.
It was held to be safer to have these by letter, in black and
white.

Of course during all these years the railways were being
improved, and better steamships being built ; the *Oceanic*,
built in 1899, 705 feet long, was the first vessel to exceed the
size of the *Great Eastern* (1858). The improvements effected,

however, were more in the way of detail than principle. A new idea was introduced by Sir Charles Parsons with his steam turbine in 1884. Here the principle of the old windmill was applied to steam. In the windmill the wind plays on the surfaces of the vanes in the sails and so turns the shaft. In the turbine a jet of steam was employed for the same purpose. The experimental boat, the *Turbinia*, can be seen at the Science Museum, London, and by 1897 this had been so improved that a record speed of 34½ knots was obtained.

At first turbines were only used in yachts and small vessels, but by 1905 they had been installed in the *Carmania*, and gave her a speed of 22 knots. The *Lusitania* and *Mauretania*, built in 1907, were also driven by turbines, and regained the " blue ribbon " of the Atlantic, which had been held by the Germans from 1897 to 1907. Everything was being speeded up.

We saw the beginning of yachting in this country in Pl. 17 , Vol. II, where we illustrated the " yaugh " which the Dutchman gave to Charles II soon after the Restoration. Pepys went to see it in 1660, and notes that Pett, the shipbuilder, was to build another to race against it. Fig. 148 in this book shows another king's yacht, the *Britannia*, which belonged to His Majesty King George V. This wonderful boat, designed by Watson of Glasgow, the great lifeboat designer of early days, was built on the Clyde by Messrs. Henderson as long ago as 1893, and, starting life as a cutter, she sailed along merrily till quite recently under a Bermuda rig.

The tricycle, as Fig. 147, dates from 1876. This was for sedate riders. The pedal levers were connected by chains to a cranked shaft which drove the large 50 inches diameter wheel. The steering handle was attached to the small front wheel, and this was linked up by a bar to the rear wheel so that both turned tangent to the curve. Elderly people could now join their young folks on the road. The cost of the machine when made was £10 13s. 2d.

The youth of the day rode on penny-farthing bicycles,

FIG. 148.—His Majesty the King's Yacht *Britannia* in Cutter Rig, 1893. (Details from contemporary photo by West & Son, Southsea.)

as Fig. 149, and it was about 1884 that the safety bicycle as we know it to-day was invented. In 1888 Dunlop patented his pneumatic tyres, which began to replace those of solid rubber, or others made with a hollow inside, which were called " cushion."

The same year (1884) that the steam turbine was invented Daimler brought out a light oil engine, and in 1885

FIG. 149.—All Out on a Penny-farthing, front wheel 58 inches diameter, 1884.

(*Science Museum, London.*)

Benz constructed his first motor-car. Fig. 150 shows an early Benz at the Science Museum, London, where is a fine collection showing the development of cars. One detail to be remembered is that the car has enabled many men to do far more work in their lives than was possible before. The country doctor and builder, to take only two examples, increased their effective radius and very much shortened the time taken on their journeys. As well, heavier loads could be carried at a more rapid rate.

FIG. 150.—First Car brought to England in 1888.
(*Science Museum, London.*)

In 1890 the first Tube railway in the world was constructed from South London to the City; the tramways
could not deal with the traffic. Some traffic was thus taken
off the streets, and one looks forward to the time when all
surface and overhead railways will be driven underground
in cities.

In 1892 Dr. Diesel invented his engine, which worked
on crude oil injected and sprayed into the cylinders under
pressure. Again, oil began to be used as fuel in the furnace
of a steam boiler. Traction on sea and land was continually
being improved.

Tubes and cars were to effect great alterations in the
social customs of the people. The old steam trains had

their first, second and third classes, and now the second has gone and only magnates ride first to-day. In the long carriages of the Tubes all classes travel together now in friendly fashion, as they do in the motor-coaches on the road. Life on the road has revived, the coaching inn has become the A.A. hotel, and friendly scouts will direct you to the innumerable cafés and roadhouses which have sprung up. The shades of marching legionaries on Watling Street are disturbed by lorries that flash along at night. Even Dick Turpin has come back as the unromantic motor bandit.

But this extension of travel has landed us into a terrible traffic problem. Think of a town whose roads once brought the farmer and his stock to market, with only an occasional passing coach, now confronted with a constant stream of motor traffic which only wants to get through quickly. This has been remedied to some extent by the provision of arterial roads dodging bottle-neck stretches, though these, if unskilfully planned or choked by ribbon development, can and have become equally congested. Then difficult towns are often by-passed, though sometimes the citizens object that they lose trade. Basingstoke, Chelmsford, Shrewsbury, among a host of others, can be thus swept round, and the Oxford by-pass is a very successful effort, in a semi-circle to the north of the city.

We have seen in our Cursory Chronicle that it was in 1897 that Burne-Jones read of Marconi's experiments with wireless. Again this was developed, until to-day it forms the most marvellous instrument for communication.

Another small detail of no apparent importance yet had its effect in the speed at which work could be done, and that was the invention of photo-prints. We started using these about 1898. Before then the architect and engineer made very careful drawings on Whatman paper. If a dozen copies were wanted these were all traced, on tracing linen or paper, one at a time, because there was only the one original. To-day one negative drawing is made in pencil, and in an hour or so the photo-printer can make dozens

FIG. 151.—Oxford Street, London.

Note the confusion of the Traffic, Architecture and Advertising.

FIG. 152A—The Last of England.

(From the Painting by Ford M—d. B—— A.d—— S—

of prints. So instructions can be given far more quickly.

The camera has helped in many other ways. At the beginning of our period paper-making, printing and illustrating had not advanced much beyond Caxton's days. The paper was made of flax, cotton or rags; the type was set up by hand, and the illustration was engraved on wood blocks. The work was good but slow, so like everything else it was speeded up. To-day forests are cut down to provide the wood-pulp for the paper, and paper and artificial silk come from the same root. Esparto grass furnishes the paper for books, which are set up by the Monotype machine, while the Linotype does the same thing for the great rotary presses which print the newspapers. For illustrating, line drawings can be photographed on to the sensitized surface of a zinc block and the background eaten away, or a photograph taken through a screen produces the half-tone block. These and many other methods are used to produce the endless variety of printed matter which is needed now.

By 1903 mechanical vehicles in England were allowed to increase their speed to twenty miles an hour, and on December 17th of the same year the Wright brothers made the first mechanically-propelled flight in an aeroplane. Some credit for this must be given to Daimler's light engine, invented in 1884, because without this the Wright brothers would not have been able to push their box kite through the air. The original Wright aeroplane is in the Science Museum, London.

The aeroplane has developed into the speediest form of transport yet invented by man, and it is difficult to imagine any method which can possibly be more speedy—unless of course one ascends into the stratosphere and ricochets round the roof of the world, or is shot through space in a rocket. Alcock and Brown took twenty-three hours on their first flight across the Atlantic in a Vickers-Vimy bomber in 1919, but the big American bombers flown across in 1941 on the Atlantic ferry service have done the trip sometimes in less than nine hours—an amazing performance. There is little doubt that in the next decade aerial crossing will largely replace the steamer passage to America, and the development of regular passenger air .travel services will extend to the furthest quarters of the globe. But something must be done to restrain the evil minded among the nations from dropping bombs on inoffensive neighbours.

Another twentieth-century accomplishment was the completion by the Americans of the Panama Canal, which de Lesseps had begun in 1879. This was long before Ronald Ross discovered the malarial parasite in 1897, so de Lesseps was defeated as much by the mosquito as by the work itself. When the Americans took the abandoned works over in 1904 the first enemy they attacked was the mosquito, and after conquering him they got to work and carried the canal to a successful conclusion, and so linked the Atlantic and Pacific.

Perhaps the most potent form of communication between the races of mankind is the film of animated pictures in which the people shown, talk. These pictures go all over the world, and their producers are judged by them. If the life depicted is noble and worthy, good will result, but if it is base and unworthy then evil will be done.

Cruising in liners must be mentioned. A love of foreign travel has grown up during our period among people who had not hitherto made the Grand Tour. Messrs. Cook, Lunn and the Polytechnic had all conducted tours abroad, at very moderate prices, and with great advantage to the travellers. Many people discovered our debt to Italy. Then the abominable financial crises made the pound abroad worth less than the pound at home. So it occurred to some bright spirit that this could be got over by travelling in a British liner, with the result that a cruise in the Mediterranean or round the Atlantic islands or the Northern capitals became quite an ordinary holiday.

What the future holds no man can say, but we think we have given enough to show our readers the marvellous developments which have taken place in transport and communication during the period which this book covers.

FIG. 153.—Coloured Costume Plate.

CHAPTER VIII

SOCIAL LIFE REFLECTED IN COSTUME

ONE great difficulty in writing about Everyday Life and Things is that, when you turn to contemporary sources, it is the extraordinary which is illustrated rather than the ordinary. There is a good tale told of an editor who assembled his reporters and instructed them that if a dog bit a man that was not " news "—but if a man bit a dog it was. From the editor's point of view this was right ; his readers, at their breakfast table, would interrupt their porridge-eating to inform the rest of the family that here was an extraordinary happening—a man had actually bitten a dog.

This must be borne in mind—men do not regularly bite dogs, or act as gangsters, or divorce their wives, or cheat, or swindle. The work of the world is carried on by decent respectable folk, who ask no more than to be able to make a living, fall in love, get married, have nice fat round babies and bring them up to be decent boys and girls ; the old man may do a little gardening during the week-end, and the wife busies herself with the home. When the supply of these nice people gives out, then civilization cracks ; but they are not " news."

These preliminary remarks can be taken as applying to ourselves. It may be that, because we detest certain aspects of Industrialism, we present to our readers a picture in which the spotlights play on children in factories and a general grubbiness. This picture would be untrue, because side by side with it there existed a very happy middle-class family life.

We suppose most boys and girls have read Lytton

Fig. 154.—A Juvenile Party, 1864.
(From " Bird's-eye Views of Modern Society," by Richard Doyle.)

FIG. 155.—At the Sea-side, 1864.
(From "Bird's-eye Views of Society," Richard Doyle.)

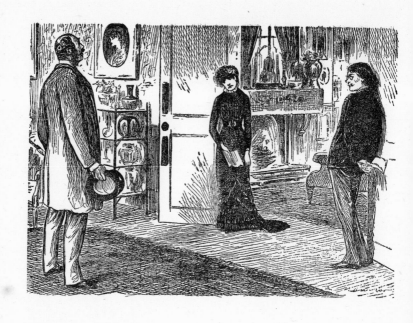

Fig. 156— Suburban Interiors in 1882
(*From the "Punch" illustrations by George Du Maurier.*)

FIG. 157.—A Garden Party in 1912.
(From a drawing by C. A. Shepperson, reproduced by permission of the Proprietors of "Punch.")

FIG. 158.—Bonnets and Hats.

Strachey's "Life of Queen Victoria." If not, they should do so, because it is a great biography. The Queen had married the man of her choice in 1840, and by 1851 the Prince Consort had shown his powers in the organization of the Great Exhibition, which was the prelude to a period of great prosperity. Part of the charm of Strachey's book is that he does not hesitate to make gentle fun of some of the Queen's peculiarities, yet in the end a picture emerges of a very great woman indeed, entirely feminine and possessed of all the Victorian virtues and an indomitable soul. So that one can hardly understand the beginning of our period (1851), unless one realizes that Victorian middle-class life was founded and modelled on the happy married life and virtues of Victoria herself.

Which brings us to this new middle class which had been called into being by the rise of Industrialism. Up till the end of the eighteenth century England had been divided— or not so much divided as arranged—into two classes, Earl and Churl, Gentle and Simple, which were based on the land. We saw the end of it in Vol. III, in the Woodforde Diary ; great landowners then, like Coke of Holkham, did actually lead the people, and agriculture was the greatest industry. With the advent of Industrialism agriculture began to decline, and by the time of the Reform Bill of 1832 the industrialists had so consolidated their position that they could, if they had so desired, have become the new leaders. But it was discovered that something fundamental was lacking in this new middle class. Industry did not appear to be able to provide a foundation on which you could build. The middle class was recruited from below, but nobody wished to remain in it. It was held to be more respectable to sell goods

Fig. 159.—Bonnets and Hats.

wholesale than retail. The thing to do was to make money and move up one; so there were many divisions in this new class, and it lost power consequently.

In the Woodforde Diary, in 1795, you read of a dinner-party at Cole, which included a saddler, a stationer and a milliner. The Woodfordes were of good professional stock—parsons and doctors, and in the nineteenth century would not have associated with tradesmen.

The saying that "the Englishman loves a lord" does not necessarily mean that he is a snob. Nor does the fact that, if you want to outrage an Englishman, you have only

195

FIG. 160.—Bonnets and Hats.

to tell him that he is "no gentleman." It may be that in his heart he agrees with Socrates, who, in Xenophon's "Oeconomicus," said that Ischomachus deserved to be called by that grand name "gentleman," because he combined goodness with beauty and truth. If this is so, it is a worthy ideal. Another interesting detail is how the lords have maintained their position. By recruitment from below, by judicious marriages, by sticking to their land and by adaptability, they remain good lords. There is an amusing Leech drawing in *Punch* for 1863 of the Aristocratic Hotel Company (Limited), in which dukes and lords are waiting on their guests, and it is illustrated as "A probable scene, if our noble lords go on dabbling in business." So the upper crust of the English pie is a good strong one, and need be to support all those who wish to climb on to it.

In dealing with the costume of our period we have drawn out a chart, Fig. 163, showing its general development, and have made smaller "cuts" giving the detail.

We will begin with A, Fig. 163, a picture of the British matron of 1851. Inside the house she ruled supreme; she was queen herself there. The husband could make the

money in the City, but
the wife looked after
the spending of it. She
was formidable and had
something of the old
Roman spirit about
her. Nobody was al-
lowed to challenge her,
and she trained her
daughters to be good
housewives. Look at
her in Fig. 165, in her
crinoline ; she stands
as safe and secure as a
pyramid, and rather re-
sembles one in outline.

Perhaps the very
best way of getting an
idea of how life was
lived during this time
is to turn over the
pages of *Punch* and
study the wonderful
drawings of John
Leech, done between
1842–64. There are

FIG. 161.—Bonnets and Hats.

the pictures produced for the pleasure of the ordinary
readers of *Punch*, showing amusing incidents in their own
scheme of life. Then other drawings which had a " news "
value. The installation of a shower-bath to-day would
not be considered sufficiently a novelty to use it as an
illustration, but *Punch* shows that it was in 1850. Again,
the people who were making money in the cities and
wished to indulge in the pleasures of the countryside were
made fun of, in a good-humoured way. " Mr. Briggs "
had a long enough purse to be able to buy a horse, but
not enough knowledge to get a good one. In fact, one

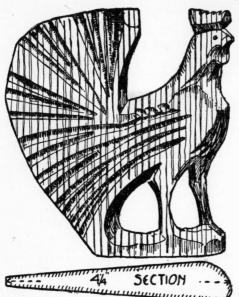

FIG. 162.—Carved Wooden Toy Animal.

of the first he did buy had been in a circus, and trained to sit down when the band played, which was awkward for Mr. Briggs when they first met a German band on the road. But nothing daunts Mr. Briggs, not even his wife—that is one of his good points—so that we soon find him fox hunting and enjoying a glorious run on his own legs, his horse having got rid of him at an early stage. Still he perseveres, and soon gets the brush (cost 10s.).

So he is shown fishing, shooting, racing and deer stalking, always making mistakes, but putting on no side, laughing at his own failures and gradually being accepted, as he and his like were if they were good fellows. They all needed clothing in the appropriate garments, and their guineas were just as acceptable to the tailors as were other people's.

1856 is a memorable year in connection with dress, because Perkin, an English chemist, discovered then that aniline dyes could be made from coal tar. These early dyes were rather crude in colour, so the Victorian matron has been accused of want of taste.

In 1858 the Volunteers were made equally good fun of in *Punch*, and especially by the small boys. That is another point. These youngsters had not yet been caught up in the net of compulsory education, so the streets swarmed with them, and they swept crossings, held horses

A. 1850~60   B. 1860~70   C. 1875

D. 1878   E. 1883   F. 1885

G. 1895   H. 1911   I. 1924   J. 1934

FIG. 163.—The Evolution of Woman's Dress between 1851 and 1934.
From 1934 on skirts have shortened again almost to the 1924 height.

O   199

FIG. 164.—Carved Wooden Toy Animal.

and generally sauced everybody. They were a real blessing to the *Punch* artists of the day and provided them with many of their jokes ; but they were poor and ragged. Many of the older figures as well might have been transferred from Cruikshanks' drawings in Egan's " Life in London " of 1821. Under the prosperity there was a substratum of squalor and misery.

Figs. 143, 154 and 155 are reproduced from drawings by Richard Doyle which first appeared in the *Cornhill Magazine* of 1861 and 1862, over the title " Bird's-eye Views of Modern Society." Judged by the pictures, it was a rich, comfortable period. The Crimean War and the Indian Mutiny were passed, and though the American Civil War had begun, and was to cause distress in our cotton industry, the other trades were very prosperous. People amused themselves by riding or driving, as Fig. 143.

The crinoline still remained, and showed the stability of woman's position. But a sad thing was to happen, and that was the death of the Prince Consort in 1861. He had formed an admirable leader for the men of science and industry, and under his continued guidance Industrialism might have proceeded on more planned lines. So far as this section is concerned, however, when her husband died, Queen Victoria withdrew herself from the public eye and lived in seclusion. As the years passed the fashionable world looked more and more to the Prince of Wales (Edward VII) and the Princess for guidance.

It is an interesting speculation what would have happened if the Prince Consort had lived as long as Queen Victoria. If this had been so, and the Queen had decided that the crinoline should be worn at Court, then it would have been worn, perhaps for another decade or so. It was absolutely typical of its time, as all dress is. Look back a little and think of dress in the Regent's time. It was as gay as the goings on of George IV and his brothers. When the nice young Queen came to the throne in 1837, dress soon reflected the change, and became simple and almost Quakerish. Women no longer wanted to look gay, but nice.

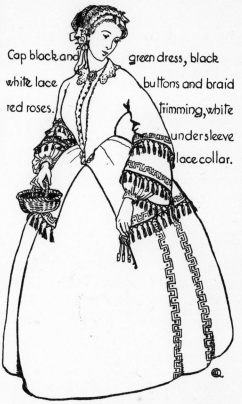

Cap black and white lace red roses.

green dress, black buttons and braid trimming, white undersleeve lace collar.

FIG. 165.—" Le Monde-élégant " (1858).

The skirts of dresses became full and, worn over many petticoats, assumed the crinoline shape, though the crinoline itself was not introduced until 1854. As it remained in use until 1866, this pyramidal form which woman gave herself lasted longer than any other fashion since. The death of the Prince Consort then, and the retirement of the Queen, mark the close of one of fashion's epochs.

The next development cannot be regarded as other than experimental. By 1866 the skirt began to be straightened in front and pulled up at the back, where it was bunched up into the bustle form, as B, Fig. 163. This was the first appearance of this feature. The skirt

Green and black hat
buff feather.

buff cloth dress
green silk frills
and waistcoat
white lace.

FIG. 166.—" The Milliner and
Dressmaker " (1870).

was still full round the bottom.

In the 'seventies we enter into the modern period of tumult and trouble, and there were many contributory causes. First, comes the Franco-Prussian War. The Crimean War had appeared reasonable; the Indian Mutiny had to be quelled; the War of Italian Unity had a cause behind it, and the Civil War was against slavery. But the Franco-Prussian War was a demonstration of the brutality of force; nothing was distinguishable in it but aggression. This awful duel between France and Germany, which still continues, was disturbing. It was almost as if a man armed with a mace, and clad in chain armour, had forced his way into a drawing-room. People began to ask what it portended.

Then the education of women began to have far-reaching effects. If we look at our Chart (pp. viii, ix) we shall find that Bedford College, London, for women, was founded in 1849, and Cheltenham College, the first boarding school for girls, in 1854. Many more followed in the 'seventies. You cannot bring many young women together and keep

Silver grey silk dress, frills and bows of silk trimmed red roses.

FIG. 167.—"The Milliner and Dressmaker" (1875).

them healthy unless you encourage them to take exercise. So games began to be played. Croquet, golf, Badminton and lawn tennis, which developed out of Badminton, all date from the 'seventies, and all needed appropriate costumes, which we illustrate.

Then these educated women began to find their way out of their sheltered homes into the world outside. Many became teachers, but some few, greatly daring, became doctors, and the London School of Medicine for Women was opened in 1874. Then the educated women began to be dissatisfied with the treatment they received. For work done equal to men they did not receive equal pay. Out in the world, they discovered the shocking conditions

Pink organdie dress with white tartan line over black silk, black silk plastrons on front of dress, black kilting piping and cuffs.

FIG. 168.—Victoria and Albert Museum (1879).

under which their poorer industrial sisters lived. Women's rights and suffrage began to be talked about, and it was not only the men who were against them. The British matron, happily married, looked on them with disfavour. From her point of view the Bible and Mrs. Beeton's Cookery Book of 1859–63 were the most important books to have in her home, and her husband was much the same. There is a good tale of an industrialist who built a house. A friend, going over it and searching for the library, asked "Where do you keep your books?" and was told by the host, "Why, at the office of course."

These simple folk only reflected the feelings of Queen Victoria. Strachey quotes a letter she wrote on seeing a report of a meeting held in favour of women's suffrage in 1870. The Queen wrote that she was anxious to enlist everyone to speak or write against this mad, wicked folly. "Lady ——" (she apparently had been at the meeting) "ought to get a good whipping."

So it can be seen that we can no longer write of security and crinolines, but must be prepared for constant changes in fashions to respond to all these varying moods. The British matron, with " Mrs. Beeton" under her arm, sways off our little stage in her crinoline, and her place is taken by the fashionable woman or the lady doctor, or any of the dozen other kinds of females who now appear.

Red velvet dress turned back white lace, train and sleeves edged lace. under dress rucked green silk.

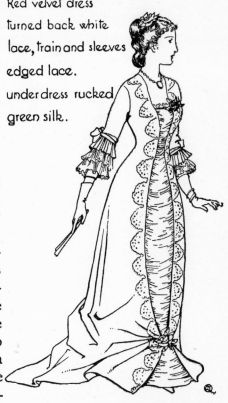

The first great alteration in dress comes about 1873. Paris always provides the models, and during the War had little time to think of dress. When it was over there came reaction and extravagance. Post-war periods are always bad

FIG. 169.—"Le Journal des Modes" (1880).

for dress design, and restraint and simplicity are wont to disappear. We see this in C, Fig. 163. The dress is closely modelled to the figure down to the hips, but the skirt is still full and has a spoon train. We think the matron of 1851 would have condemned it as frilly and frivolous.

D, Fig. 163, shows that by 1878 the tight fitting of the dress had been continued down to the knees ; there was a fall of material at the back and a spoon train. The dresses, however, were graceful and pretty.

Now for the reaction to this. Turn to our chart, and you will find that in the 'eighties, judged by the foundations of societies for good causes, more of these came into being

Maroon
voile dress
white collar
and cuffs

pleated satin
front and buttons
16 yds. material.

FIG. 170.—" Myra's Journal " (1883).

in this decade than ever before or since. You will find this reflected in E, Fig. 163. Woman, after all, dresses to please her menfolk, not herself. If they wish her to be gay and frivolous, she will be so ; but if they wish her to go to a Fabian meeting, she asks for a moment in which to change her dress. In the 'seventies woman showed that she had a beautiful figure ; in the early 'eighties she concealed it under bunchiness.

As the decade progressed, however, other things happened. Gold was discovered on the Rand in 1884, and money began to be made in S. Africa and find its way to England. By 1884 sleeves were puffed at the shoulder, and skirts cut to ankle length for walking. By 1885 the full bustle had come in again, as F, Fig. 163, which looks as if the fashion artists were encouraging their clients to extravagance.

So we pass to the gay 'nineties, when dress was very decorated and not at all beautiful. The sleeves were very full, and the skirts were belled (G, Fig. 163). Against this, however, was the fact that the safety bicycle had been invented in 1884, and was beginning to be used by women. The boneshaker of 1868, as Fig. 146, had been for the brothers, and an adventurous sister, before she left school, might have tried her luck on it in the garden, but would not have dared to do so in the road, and the penny-farthing, of course, was never for her.

Lawn tennis and the safety bicycle have contributed more to women's happiness and freedom than any other two things that were ever invented. Before they arrived, the well-to-do woman could hunt or drive, but her poorer sisters could not do much more than go for a walk. With lawn tennis a good game with young men was possible, and though it was rather patball, still it made the garden parties jollier. With

White muslin dress trimmed Torchon lace.

FIG. 171.—At Victoria and Albert Museum (1885).

the safety bicycle, picnics and rides into the country became possible for those who could not afford a horse.

Then, by the Act of 1896 mechanically-propelled vehicles were allowed to move on the roads at twelve miles an hour, and the motor came into its own, but for many years it was only a plaything for the rich. Still it needed new costumes, and the women muffled themselves up in veils to keep the dust from the untarred roads out of their hair.

It is rather difficult to find an explanation for dress at the beginning of the twentieth century. Gradually the skirts became tighter and the sleeves less full, and enormous

Bonnet of velvet trimmed lace and ostrich feathers.

Jacket of brown corduroy velvet. painted mussel-shell buttons. brown cloth dress.

FIG. 172.—Walking Dress (1885).

hats were worn. By 1911 the skirts were so tight that active young women did actually hobble instead of walk. Perhaps they wished to give the impression that they could be captured very easily. One of the authors, forgetting her hobble, dashed upstairs one day and split her skirt to her knees, and women were not supposed to have knees then. You see the type in Fig. 174.

Then the War came on, and all elaboration ceased. Women wore uniform, and when they got out of it wanted dresses which would slip over their heads and give them a dressed feeling with the minimum of trouble, as I, Fig. 163 ; and the skirts got shorter and shorter, until everybody realized that women had knees.

By 1926 the skirts began to lengthen, until to-day the evening dress trails once more on the floor, to the inconvenience of the attendant male. Women, however, demand more freedom for their bodies, and are less corseted now than ever before.

Bonnets are an interesting study. The matron of 1851 might have, as a young girl, indulged in a hat, pork-pie or otherwise, but the moment she married she donned the bonnet as a symbol of the happy state in which she found herself, and this remained so till the late 'eighties. Since then it has become difficult to distinguish grandmamma from granddaughter.

blue dress, mauve bands, rosettes, and zouave

mauve & blue

white silk blouse and sleeves. blue hat & mauve feather

At the beginning of our period people were still content with clothes made of the woven fibres of wool, hair, cotton, flax or silk. The fabrics continued to be produced on much the same lines as those described in Vol. III, though

FIG. 173.—" Journal des Modes " (1893).

there were improvements in the details of the machinery. The biggest modern development has been in the production of artificial silk or rayon. With real silk the silkworm eats mulberry leaves, and then, when it forms its chrysalis, extrudes from itself these vegetable fibres to form the silk covering to the cocoon. It then occurred to the chemist to follow the worm's example. He cut down trees and turned these into a fibrous pulp, which he extruded from a machine as a thread—and as a result Jill can be as well dressed as her mistress.

And what of the men? Well, very little can be said

COLOUR

Mauve chiffon scarf goldcord girdle.

Yellow ninon tunic with écru lace over yellow satin dress, small train. very narrow skirt.

FIG. 174.—From "Weldon's Ladies' Journal" (1911).

for them sartorially. Under Industrialism, year by year they have become greyer and greyer. When young they still break out occasionally into colour. Socks and ties may attract their attention, and golfers at times seemed to be possessed of a sense of adventure. Only the soldiers and sailors in their full dress serve to remind the women of those good old days when man, like the cock pheasant, was the dinkier bird.

Still men have this consolation— they can watch their womenfolk's attempts in the direction of dress. If they like them, the simple and ingenuous creatures will consult their menfolk and demand, "How do you like my new hat ? Do you think this trimming goes well ? Does my skirt hang nicely ? " All of which is very pleasant and nice, and part of woman's charm.

Now we come to our conclusion. This is the eleventh book, and finishes the series we have been writing during the last nineteen years. All these have been addressed to boys and girls of fourteen to eighteen, and we have tried to show men and women at work throughout the Ages. We hoped that our readers might pick up ideas and be able

to say to them-
selves, "Ah, that
job would suit me
—I should like to
do that." To like
your work is im-
portant. Supposing
Pasteur had found
himself compelled
to work at a moving
assembly line, and
Lister to serve be-
hind a counter.
They would have
been unhappy, and
we should have lost
the benefit of their
real work.

So it is a good
idea to hunt around
for interesting work
—but work be-
comes more me-
chanical and less
interesting. Still,

FIG. 175.—Bathing Dresses.
1885.   Present Day

need this be so? If you regard it as a duty to treat your
neighbour as yourself, this would seem to carry with it the
obligation to make work not only profitable, but pleasant.

Again, a boy or girl may say, "I am not a Pasteur or
Lister"—but how can you be sure? We may have sacrificed many in our worship of the machine. There remains
this consolation: if we can't all be great, we can be good
citizens and play our part in life as fairly and decently as
in a game of cricket (without too much leg theory).

THE END

INDEX TO TEXT

Note.—The ordinary figures denote references to pages of **text**, those in black type the illustrations.

INDEX

INDEX